This New
Book of Saints
is dedicated to
Saint Joseph
Patron
of the
Universal Church

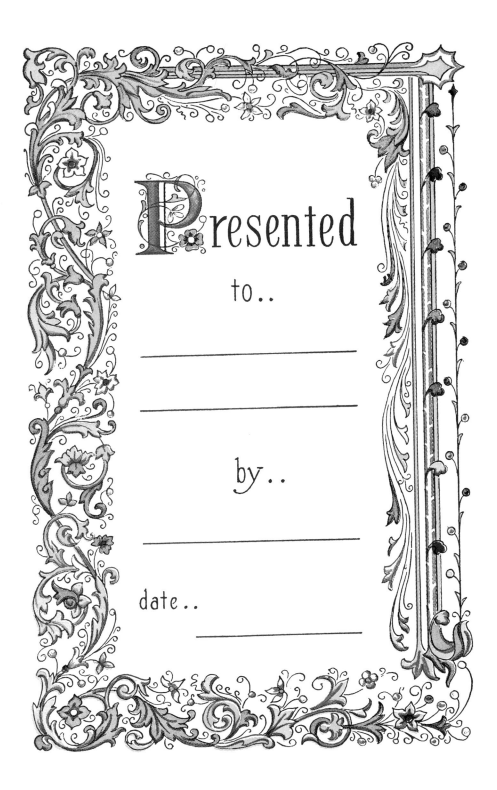

Presented

to..

_____

_____

by..

_____

date..

_____

"Blessed be God in His Angels and in His Saints"

New
PICTURE
BOOK OF SAINTS

SAINT JOSEPH EDITION

ILLUSTRATED LIVES
OF THE SAINTS
FOR YOUNG AND OLD

By

REV. LAWRENCE G. LOVASIK, S.V.D.

Divine Word Missionary

CATHOLIC BOOK PUBLISHING COMPANY
NEW YORK

FOREWORD

My dear friend,

In the Apostles' Creed you say, "I believe in the communion of saints." This means the union of the faithful on earth, the blessed in heaven, and the souls in purgatory, with Christ as their Head. The word "saints" means all those in the state of sanctifying grace. Therefore, you have millions of friends, bound to you by the spiritual bond of divine grace and charity flowing from Christ, our divine Head. These friends are especially the saints in heaven who are now enjoying their triumph with God forever. They are members of the Church Triumphant, and the Church honors all of them on the Feast of All Saints, November 1.

Through the communion of saints, the blessed in heaven can help you on earth by praying for you. Above all, the Queen of Saints, Mary, Mother of God and Our Mother, is praying for you before the throne of her Son. As one of the faithful on earth, through the communion of saints, you should honor the saints in heaven and pray to them, because they are worthy of honor, and as friends of God will help you to serve God and save your soul.

I have prepared these life stories of the saints and these wonderful pictures in color to help you to know the saints better. They are your brothers and sisters in heaven. They want to help you get to heaven. Try to be like the saints in doing all you can to know, love and serve God as they did, and in this way save your soul. Ask the saints to help you to practice virtue and to overcome sin.

God wants you, too, to become a saint. You do not have to be canonized to become a saint. You can be a saint by doing God's will at all times. This means loving God with all your heart, and your neighbor as yourself for the love of God.

Your friend in Jesus and Mary and the Saints,

FATHER LAWRENCE G. LOVASIK, S.V.D.

NIHIL OBSTAT: Daniel V. Flynn, J.C.D. — *Censor Librorum*
IMPRIMATUR: Joseph T. O'Keefe
Vicar General, Archdiocese of New York
(T-235)

TABLE OF CONTENTS

CONTENTS — CONTINUED

OUR LADY, QUEEN OF ALL SAINTS

August 22

O God, You have given us the Mother of Your Son to be our Mother and Queen. Through her intercession, grant that we may attain the glory destined for Your adopted children in Your heavenly Kingdom.

AFTER a most holy life and death the Blessed Virgin Mary was gloriously assumed into heaven with soul and body and was crowned Queen of Heaven by her own Son.

Mary is Queen because her Son is the Second Person of the Blessed Trinity, and as man He is King and Lord of all creation. Jesus is our King because He redeemed us. The Blessed Virgin is our Queen because she had a very special part in our redemption, in our Lord's struggle with His enemies and in His victory over them; she therefore has a share in His royal dignity.

As Mary took part in the Incarnation and Redemption by her Divine Motherhood and her sorrows on Calvary, so she now helps in giving to people the graces merited by her Son. St. Bernard says, "It is the will of God that we should have all things through Mary." The saints also have received the graces they needed to become saints through her prayers. All the virtues they practiced are to be found in her in a very wonderful way. She is truly the Queen of All Saints. On October 11, 1954, Pope Pius XII instituted the Feast of the Queenship of Mary in the liturgical calendar of the Church.

SAINT FRANCES CABRINI

November 13

O God, through the work of St. Frances Cabrini You brought comfort and love to the immigrants and those in need. May her example and work be continued in the lives of those dedicated to You.

Patron of Emigrants

FRANCES Cabrini was born in Italy in 1850, one of thirteen children. When she was eighteen years old, poor health kept her from becoming a Sister. She helped her mother and father until their death, and then worked on a farm with her brother and sister.

A priest asked her to teach in a girls' school. She stayed there for six years. At the request of the bishop she started a missionary order in honor of the Sacred Heart of Jesus to care for poor children in hospitals and schools.

Frances wrote to Pope Leo XIII, and he told her, "Go to the United States, my child. There is much work awaiting you there."

She came to the United States with six Sisters in 1889, and began working among the Italian people of New York. She became an American citizen. Mother Cabrini traveled very much. She founded many orphanages, schools, and hospitals not only in the United States but throughout Europe.

Mother Cabrini was the first American citizen to become a saint. She was canonized by Pope Pius XII on July 7, 1946.

ANTHONY was born in the year 251 in Egypt. He wanted to fulfill the words of our Lord: "If thou wilt be perfect, go, sell, what thou hast, and give to the poor." While still a young man, he gave away all his possessions and begged an old hermit to teach him how to live a holy life. He visited a number of hermits and tried to imitate their example. He retired into the desert, where he lived the life of a hermit for many years. He devoted himself to prayer and penance.

For more than twenty years Anthony was tempted by the devil, but he overcame temptation by prayer and sacrifice. Many people flocked to him for advice. He consented to guide them in holiness. In this way he founded the first monastery, so that he is called the father of monastic life and the patriarch of monks.

His miracles drew so many people to him that he fled again into the desert, where he lived by hard work and prayer. St. Athanasius, who wrote his life story, said that just knowing about the way Anthony lived is a good guide to virtue.

In 305, Anthony founded a religious community of hermits who lived in separate cells. He died in 356 at the age of one hundred and five.

SAINT ANTHONY THE ABBOT

January 17

Lord God, You gave St. Anthony the Abbot the grace of serving in the desert in prayer with You. Aided by his intercession, may we practice self-denial and hence always love You above all things.

Patron of Gravediggers

S EBASTIAN was the son of wealthy parents. He became the captain of the soldiers who guarded the Roman Emperor.

The Emperor made the Christians suffer very much. Sebastian helped them by visiting them in prison, bringing them money, clothing and food.

Once Sebastian healed a soldier's wife by making the Sign of the Cross over her. Both she and her husband asked to be baptized. He also converted a governor at Rome and many others.

Sebastian was accused of being a Christian and was to be put to death. He was tied, and soldiers shot arrows at him. That night a Christian woman, thinking he was dead, had some men bring the martyr to her home and prepare his body for burial. But Sebastian was still alive. She cared for him until he was well again.

Sebastian went back to see the Emperor and begged him to be kind to the Christians. But the Emperor ordered soldiers to kill Sebastian. After his death, the martyr appeared to a holy woman and told her where his body might be found. His body was then brought to the catacombs and buried there.

SAINT SEBASTIAN

January 20

O Lord, grant us a spirit of strength. Taught by the glorious example of Your Martyr St. Sebastian, may we learn how to obey You rather than men.

Patron of Athletes
and Soldiers

SAINT AGNES

January 21

All-powerful and ever-living God, You choose the weak in this world to confound the powerful. As we celebrate the anniversary of the martyrdom of St. Agnes, may we like her remain constant in faith.

Patron of Children of Mary

AGNES was only twelve years old when she was led to the altar of the pagan goddess Minerva in Rome to offer incense to her. But she raised her hands to Jesus Christ and made the Sign of the Cross.

The soldiers bound her hands and feet. Her young hands were so thin that the chains slipped from her wrists. When the judge saw that she was not afraid of pain, he had her clothes stripped off, and she had to stand in the street before a pagan crowd. She cried out, "Christ will guard His own."

While the crowd turned away from her, a young man dared to look at her with sinful thoughts. A flash of lightning struck him blind.

Agnes was offered the hand of a rich young man in marriage, but she answered, "Christ is my Spouse. He chose me first and His I will be. He made my soul beautiful with the jewels of grace and virtue. I belong to Him whom the angels serve."

After having prayed, she bowed her neck to the sword. At one stroke her head was cut off, and the angels took her soul to heaven.

The name Agnes comes from the Latin word *agnus,* meaning lamb, and reminds us of the gentleness of this young saint.

SAINT FRANCIS DE SALES

January 24

Father in heaven, You prompted St. Francis de Sales to become all things to all men for the salvation of men. May his example inspire us to dedicated love in the service of our brothers.

Patron of Writers

FRANCIS was born in a castle in France in 1567. When he was baptized, his mother said, "Now, my son, you are the friend of the angels, the brother of Jesus, the temple of the Holy Spirit, and a member of the Church. Now you must belong to God forever."

When Francis was nine years old, he received Holy Communion often. He said, "Jesus is the teacher of holiness. I go to Him because I want Him to teach me how to become a saint. Of what use to me is all I learn in school if I do not become holy?"

Francis became a lawyer. One day he heard a voice saying to him, "Leave all and follow Me." Obeying God's call, he said, "I want to go everywhere to look for the poor and the sinners so that I may win them for Jesus."

Francis became a priest and brought many back to God by his preaching and his kindness. Later he became the bishop of Geneva. He wrote many books, and that is the reason why he is honored as the patron of spiritual writers. Together with St. Jane Frances de Chantal he founded the Order of the Visitation. He died in 1622.

16

SAINT JOHN BOSCO

January 31

God of mercy, You called St. John Bosco to be a father and teacher of the young. Grant that inspired by his ardent charity we may serve You alone and never tire of bringing others to Your Kingdom.

Patron of Editors

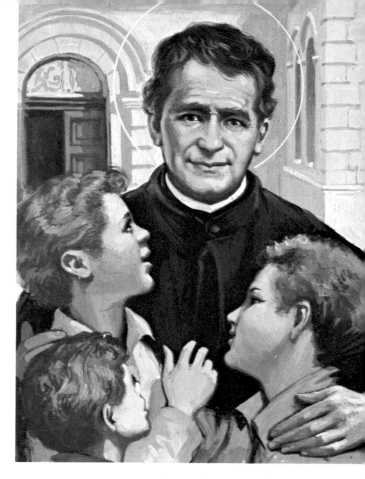

WHEN he was a boy, John learned many tricks by watching circus men. He gathered boys around him and put on little shows. Then he repeated the sermon he had heard in church.

At thirteen John left home and went to work with a farmer, then a tailor, a baker, a shoemaker, and a carpenter. In this way he worked himself through college and seminary, and became a priest.

Boys loved Father John. He found places for them to meet, to play and pray. When neighbors complained about the noise, Father John rented an old barn in a field. He called it "The Oratory." He started many of these oratories. He believed that prayer and the sacraments are the best ways of making boys good.

Don Bosco also founded the religious order of Salesians, a group of priests who would help him in his work for boys. They went also to other countries to educate boys. Father John set up shops of all kinds to teach boys different trades. He wrote many booklets and the boys printed them and sent them out for people to read.

Father John died at the age of seventy-three in 1888.

BERNADETTE'S parents were very poor. They lived near Lourdes, in France.

One day, in 1858, while Bernadette was gathering firewood, a beautiful Lady stood in a cave before her. She was dressed in blue and white, and there were roses at her feet. She smiled at Bernádette and asked her to say the rosary with her.

Bernadette saw the Lady eighteen times. Once the Lady said, "I do not promise to make you happy in this world, but in heaven."

Large crowds followed Bernadette to the grotto to say the rosary with her. They could not see the Lady.

The Lady asked Bernadette to scrape the earth. The miraculous spring of Lourdes started to flow. Many pilgrims have been cured.

When Bernadette asked the Lady her name, the Lady looked up to heaven and said, "I am the Immaculate Conception." Her message was: "Pray for sinners." She asked that a chapel be built near the grotto. Today this spot is a great shrine of the Blessed Virgin Mary.

Later, Bernadette became a nun. Her life was one of joyful suffering. She died at the age of thirty-six.

SAINT BERNADETTE

February 18

O God, protector and lover of the humble, You bestowed upon Your servant, Bernadette, the favor of beholding the Immaculate Virgin Mary and of talking with her. Grant that we may deserve to behold You in heaven.

SAINT GABRIEL OF OUR LADY OF SORROWS

February 27

O God, You taught St. Gabriel to dwell upon the sorrows of Your most sweet Mother, and rasied him to the glory of holiness and miracles. Grant that we may also share her sorrows and be saved by her protection.

Patron of Clerics

G ABRIEL was born at Assisi, March 1, 1838, the eleventh of thirteen children. He was devoted to the pleasures of the world, but, guided by Our Lady into the Passionist Order, he became a true apostle of her sorrows.

There was nothing extraordinary about him except his faithfulness to prayer, his love of sacrifice, and his joyful spirit. At the age of twenty-three, just as he was finishing his studies for the priesthood, he was stricken with tuberculosis, and died a year later at Isola on February 27, 1862.

There were no miraculous events in his life, but after his death many miracles occurred at his tomb.

He is called St. Gabriel of the Sorrowful Mother because of his great love for Mary suffering with her Son.

Remembering Jesus and Mary in their sufferings made Gabriel all the more generous in proving his love. Imitate this youthful saint by thinking frequently of the sorrows of Mary, that through her motherly care you may reach holiness and save your soul.

SAINT THOMAS AQUINAS

January 28

Father of wisdom, You inspired St. Thomas Aquinas with an ardent desire for holiness and study of sacred doctrine. Help us, we pray, to understand what he taught and to imitate what he lived.

Patron of Catholic Schools

THOMAS, the Count of Aquino, in Italy, left the University of Naples to live with the Dominican priests. His two brothers brought him back and locked him in a castle for almost two years to keep him from returning to the monastery.

The Pope called Thomas to Rome to talk with him. He commanded his mother and his brothers not to stand in the way of his vocation. Thomas went back to the Dominicans, who sent him to study in France and Germany.

Thomas became a priest and a great teacher. He wrote many books about the teachings of the Catholic Church. Known for his great love of Jesus in the Blessed Sacrament, he wrote prayers and hymns which the Church uses today to honor the Holy Eucharist.

While Thomas was praying before a large crucifix, our Lord spoke to him: "Thomas, you have written well of Me. What do you want in return?" Thomas answered, "Lord, I want nothing else but You." He died at the age of forty-seven in 1274.

SAINT
JOHN
OF GOD

March 8

O God, You filled St. John with the spirit of compassion. Grant that by practicing works of charity we may deserve to be numbered among the elect in Your Kingdom.

Patron of Book-sellers
and Heart Patients

JOHN was born in Portugal in 1495. He was a shepherd-boy until he was twenty-two years of age. For eighteen years he was a soldier in many parts of Europe. Even though he led a wild life, he loved the poor and the suffering.

John was over forty years old when he left the army in order to make up for his sins. He went back to Spain and rented a house. In it he gathered all the sick, the poor and the homeless of the town of Granada. Often carrying them there on his own back, he washed them and dressed their sores, and begged food for them. He brought many sinners back to God.

Kind people began to help him in his work. The Order which he founded grew. It became known as the Hospitaller Order of St. John of God. His motto was: "Labor without stopping; do all the good works you can while you still have the time."

After saving a man from drowning, John became very ill. On March 8, 1550, the nurses found him kneeling before a crucifix, his face resting on the feet of Jesus. He was dead.

SAINT GREGORY THE GREAT

September 3

O God, You look upon Your people with compassion and rule them with love. Through the intercession of Pope St. Gregory, give wisdom to the leaders of Your Church that the growth of Your people in holiness may be the everlasting joy of our pastors. ___

Patron of Choir Boys and Singers

GREGORY was born in the year 540. He was the son of a wealthy Roman senator; his mother was St. Silvia. Gregory's father sent him to the best teachers. He was always humble.

Gregory was prefect of Rome for one year. Then he sold all his property and used the money to build six monasteries in Sicily and one in Rome, where he went to live as a monk. He continued his kind deeds to help the needy.

One day he saw some slave children being offered for sale near the Roman Forum. On being told they were Angles from England, Gregory replied, "Not Anglcs, but Angels shall they be. The true Faith must be brought to them." Obtaining permission from the Pope, he began his journey as a missionary to England. The people of Rome later asked the Pope to recall him. After Gregory was elected Pope, he sent St. Augustine and a company of monks to England in 597. He also sent missionaries to France, Spain and Africa.

Pope Gregory is called Doctor of the Church because of the many books he wrote, especially on the liturgy of the Mass and the Office. He made wise laws to govern the Church. He died in the year 604.

L OUISE was born on August 15, 1591. Her husband died thirteen years after their marriage, leaving Louise with a son. Saint Vincent de Paul was her confessor.

Vincent organized groups of men and women to help the poor and the sick in each parish, and from them, with the help of Louise de Marillac, sprang the establishment of the Daughters of Charity of St. Vincent de Paul, dedicated to the bodily and spiritual service of the poor. Louise drew up a rule of life for the growing community. Ten years later, this religious family was approved by the Church. Vincent said that the chapel of the Sisters is the parish church, their cloister the streets of the city and the wards of the hospitals.

Vincent found in Louise a woman of clear mind, great courage, and marvelous self-sacrifice in spite of her feeble health. She was most willing to humble herself in doing works of charity. Louise was always motherly in dealing with the Sisters as well as the poor and the sick. In her last days she said to her grieving Sisters: "Be diligent in serving the poor. Love the poor, honor them, my children, as you would honor Christ Himself." She died on March 15, 1660.

SAINT LOUISE DE MARILLAC

March 15

O God, You inspired St. Louise to strive for perfect charity and so attain Your Kingdom at the end of her pilgrimage on earth. Strengthen us through her intercession that we may advance rejoicing in the way of love.

ST. PATRICK was born in Scotland in the year 387. At sixteen he was captured by pirates and sold as a slave to a chief in Ireland. While tending sheep in the mountains, he prayed constantly.

After six years, a voice from heaven told him to go back to his own country. But first he went to Rome, where he became a priest. He was then sent to England where he labored for the Church for some time. He wanted, however, to return to Ireland, and he begged the Pope to send him there. The Pope made him a bishop and then sent him as a missionary to Ireland.

One of the pagan kings of Ireland arrested Patrick. When he saw the miracles worked by Patrick, he said, "Tell us about your God. He has given you great power."

"There is but one God," answered Patrick, "and three divine Persons: the Father, the Son, and the Holy Spirit." Picking up a green shamrock he said, "Even as there are three leaves on this one stem, so there are three Persons in one God." Thereafter, he was allowed to preach the new Faith everywhere in Ireland.

SAINT PATRICK

March 17

O God, You sent St. Patrick to preach Your glory to the Irish people. Through his merits and intercession grant that we who have the honor of bearing the name of Christians may constantly proclaim Your wonderful designs to men.

———

Patron of Ireland

SAINT JOSEPH

March 19

Almighty God, You entrusted to the faithful care of Joseph the beginnings of the mysteries of man's salvation. Through his intercession may Your Church always be faithful in her service so that Your designs will be fulfilled.

Patron of a Happy Death and of the Universal Church

THE Heavenly Father chose Joseph a young carpenter of Nazareth to be the foster father of Jesus and the husband of the Blessed Virgin Mary. After they were betrothed an angel appeared to Joseph in a dream and told him that Mary would bear a Child who would be the Son of God.

Mary and Joseph had to travel to Bethlehem to register for the census. They could find no place to stay except in a stable. There Mary brought forth her Son and laid Him in a manger.

At the word of an angel Joseph took Jesus and Mary to Egypt and stayed there till the angel told him to go back to Nazareth.

When Jesus was twelve years old he was lost in Jerusalem. For three days Mary and Joseph looked for Him with great sorrow and found Him in the Temple.

At Nazareth Joseph worked hard for Jesus and Mary. Later, Jesus also worked along with Joseph in the carpenter shop and obeyed him. Joseph died in the arms of Jesus and Mary.

SAINT
BENEDICT

July 11

O God, You established
St. Benedict the Abbot
as an admirable teach-
er in the school of Di-
vine servitude. Teach
us never to prefer any-
thing to Your love and
always to run the way
of Your Command-
ments with most gener-
ous dispositions.

———

Patron against Poisoning

BENEDICT was born in the year 480. He belonged to a noble family of Rome. He went to a town called Subiaco, set on a mountain forty miles from Rome. There he lived in a cave in the side of a cliff for three years. Sometimes a raven brought him food.

Men began flocking to Benedict. Soon more than one hundred and forty monks were living with him in a monastery at Subiaco. They were busy every day praying, clearing the land, planting crops, teaching school, feeding the poor. Their motto was: "Pray and work."

Benedict and his monks built a large monastery on Monte Cassino, on the top of the mountain. It became the home of thousands of monks. Later they went out to convert the world. For centuries they were the teachers of Europe. They were called Benedictines.

Benedict had the power of miracles. Once he raised a dead boy to life.

He had a twin sister, named Scholastica, who became a nun and a great saint. She founded the Benedictine Sisters.

Benedict died near the altar where he received the Blessed Sacrament, while his monks held up his arms in prayer.

SAINT ISIDORE THE FARMER

May 15

O God, through the intercession of St. Isidore the holy Farmer grant that we may overcome all feelings of pride. May we always serve You with that humility which pleases You, through his merits and example.

Patron of Farmers

ISIDORE was born in Madrid, Spain, in the twelfth century. He was a farmer on the land of a certain wealthy nobleman of Madrid He never missed daily Mass. The neighbors accused him, to his employer, of neglecting his work in order to hear Mass, but Isidore replied, "I know, Sir, that I am your servant, but I have another Master as well, to whom I owe service and obedience."

The employer went to the farm one morning very early. When he found out that Isidore did not begin his work until a later hour, he went toward him to scold him. But he was surprised to find two strangers, each with a team of white oxen, ploughing, one on each side of Isidore. When he approached them, they disappeared. He said to Isidore, "Tell me, who are these two men who were ploughing with you just now?" Isidore said, "I have not seen any person. I ask no help from anyone but God each morning at Holy Mass." The nobleman understood that the two men he had seen were angels sent by God to help His servant, in return for his hearing Mass faithfully.

27

SAINT GABRIEL THE ARCHANGEL

September 29

O God, from the ranks of all the angels You chose the Archangel Gabriel to announce the mystery of Your Incarnation. Grant that we, who honor him on earth, may experience the effect of his patronage in heaven.

———

Patron of Communication Workers

ACCORDING to the Prophet Daniel, it was Gabriel the Archangel who announced to him the time of the coming of the Messias. He appeared to Zachary "standing on the right side of the altar of incense," as St. Luke says, to make known the future birth of John the Baptist.

Gabriel's greatest honor was to be sent to Mary at Nazareth and to announce to her that she was to be the Mother of God. Upon her consent, "The Word was made flesh and dwelt among us."

Gabriel's name means "the strength of God." He is used as a messenger in the work that shows the power and glory of God. Some of the Fathers of the Church say that he was with Jesus in His agony. He is the Angel of the Incarnation, of consolation, and of mercy.

Through many centuries Gabriel has been honored by Christians. His picture is often seen, especially as he appeared to Our Lady.

Since Gabriel left us the first words of the "Hail Mary," ask him to help you to say your rosary with true devotion.

SAINT ISIDORE OF SEVILLE

April 4

O Lord, hear our prayers, which we offer on the feast of St. Isidore. May Your Church be instructed by his teaching and benefit by his intercession.

ISIDORE was born at Cartagena in Spain. His two brothers, Leander and Fulgentius, both bishops, and his sister Florentina, are saints. As a boy Isidore was discouraged because he failed in his studies, and he ran away from school. Later he decided to go back and try again. With the help of God, he became one of the most learned men of his time.

Isidore helped in converting the leader of the Arian party, and delivered Spain from this heresy. Following a call from God, he became a hermit even though his friends pleaded with him. After his brother's death he became the Archbishop of Seville. As a teacher, ruler, founder, and reformer, he labored not only in his own diocese, but throughout Spain, and even in foreign countries. He presided at the Fourth Council of Toledo.

Isidore wrote many books. He governed his diocese about thirty-seven years. He died in Seville on April 4, 636, and within sixteen years of his death was declared a Doctor of the Church.

SAINT VINCENT FERRER

April 5

O God, You raised up St. Vincent, Your Priest, to serve You in preaching the Gospel, and to proclaim the coming of Christ to judge the world. Grant that we may attain to the joy of heaven, and there see Christ enthroned in glory.

———

Patron of Builders

VINCENT was born at Valencia in Spain in 1350. At the age of eighteen he was professed in the Order of St. Dominic. He became a doctor of Sacred Theology. He refused to accept any ecclesiastical dignities and devoted himself to missionary work. He preached in nearly every province of Spain. He preached also in France, Italy, Germany, Holland, England, Scotland and Ireland. Numerous conversions followed his preaching, which God Himself assisted by the gift of miracles. He was even invited to Mohammedan Granada. where he preached the Gospel with much success. He is considered one of the most famous missionaries of the fourteenth century.

Vincent's outstanding virtues were humility and the spirit of prayer, which made his work successful. His motto was: "Whatever you do, think not of yourself, but of God." In this spirit he preached, and God spoke through him. Though the Church was then divided by the great Schism and there were two claimants to the Papacy, the saint was honorably received by all. His wonderful missionary work lasted twenty-one years. He died on April 5, 1419.

SAINT LEO THE GREAT

November 10

*O God, You establish-
ed Your Church on the
solid rock of St. Peter
and You will never al-
low the powers of hell
to dominate her. Grant
that she may persevere
in Your truth and en-
joy continual peace
through the interces-
sion of Pope St. Leo.*

LEO was born in Tuscany in Italy. He reigned as Pope from 440 to 461. At this time Attila, called the Scourge of God, with his hordes of Huns invaded Italy. Having conquered the city of Aquileia after a three-year siege, Attila marched toward Rome. Moved with pity for the suffering people, Leo went out to meet him. Leo's plead-ings persuaded the invader to leave Rome untouched.

People wanted to know how the humble conduct of the Pope could change Attila's mind. Attila declared that, while Leo addressed him, he had become frightened at the sight of a person in priestly robes who stood nearby with bared sword, threatening his life should he disobey Leo's commands. Leo was devoted to St. Peter.

Later, when Genseric entered Rome, Leo's sanctity and eloquence again saved the city. Seeing the heresies which were attacking the Church, Leo called the Council of Chalcedon and condemned them. The Council exclaimed, "Peter has spoken by the mouth of Leo."

The holy Pontiff built many churches. He left many letters and writings of great historical value. Pope St. Leo, surnamed the Great, a Doctor of the Church, died on April 11, 461.

31

SAINT GEMMA GALGANI

April 11

O God, hear our prayers through the intercession of St. Gemma, Your Servant, that, by imitating her love for the Passion of Your loving Son, we may grow in our own love of Jesus Crucified.

———

Patron of Pharmacists

GEMMA was born near Lucca, Italy, in 1878. When she was twenty years old she was attacked by an incurable tuberculosis of the spine. After many novenas to St. Gabriel of the Sorrowful Mother, she was completely cured.

Gemma tried to imitate St. Gabriel by becoming a Passionist nun, but was rejected. She was again stricken with an illness.

Her life of love and suffering came to an end in great misery and loneliness. She said, "O Jesus, I can bear no more. If it be Your holy Will, take me." She lifted her eyes to a picture of Our Lady and said, "Mother, I commend my soul into your hands; do ask Jesus to be merciful to me."

Gemma's remains are in the chapel of the Passionist Sisters in Lucca. A marble tablet states: "Gemma Galgani from Lucca, most pure virgin, being in her twenty-fifth year, died of consumption, but was more consumed by the fire of divine love than by her wasting disease. On the eleventh of April, 1903, the vigil of Easter, her soul took its flight to the bosom of her heavenly Spouse. O beautiful soul, in the company of the Angels!"

BENEDICT Joseph Labré was born in France in 1748. He received a good education under the care of his pious parents and his uncle, a priest in the town of his birth. He loved the Bible, and for the rest of his life always carried a copy with him.

At the age of sixteen he tried to join the Trappists, but was rejected. He then tried the Carthusians and remained six weeks among them. But it turned out that this was not his vocation. He took then to the life of a pilgrim, and in this he sanctified himself, living on alms and practicing severe poverty.

Benedict made pilgrimages to many of the great shrines of Europe. The last years of his life he spent in Rome, where he made pilgrimages to different sanctuaries. In all his travels he tried to keep before him the sufferings of Jesus and Mary. His favorite Church was that of Our Lady of the Mountains in Rome. There in 1783 he was taken suddenly ill and died while those attending him said the invocation of the litany of the dying: "Holy Mary, pray for him."

Let us learn from the life of St. Benedict Joseph to remember that we are always in the presence of God, especially in church.

SAINT BENEDICT LABRE

April 16

O God, by Your grace St. Benedict Joseph persevered in imitating Christ in His poverty and humility. Through his intercession, grant that we may faithfully follow our vocation and reach that perfection which You held out to us in Your Son.

SAINT GEORGE

April 23

O Lord, we acclaim Your might and humbly pray. Just as St. George imitated the Lord's Passion, so let him now come to the aid of our weakness.

———

Patron of England and
Boy Scouts

S AINT George is one of the great martyrs of the early Church. He was a soldier and rose to high rank in the Roman Army.

The Emperor Diocletian honored George for his great bravery. When George became a Christian, he resigned his position in the army, and rebuked the Emperor himself for being so cruel to the Christians. He was put into prison and tortured, but nothing could make him change his mind. He was beheaded about the year 303.

The Christians took his body to Palestine. Pilgrimages were made later to his tomb in the Holy Land, and many miracles were worked through his prayers before God.

The figure of St. George and the Dragon is a symbol of his Christian courage in overcoming the spirit of evil, the devil, who in the Bible is called the dragon.

St. George was chosen as patron saint of England by the first Norman kings, and in the thirteenth century his feast was declared a public holiday.

SAINT MARK THE EVANGELIST

April 25

God our Father, You helped St. Mark the Evangelist with Your grace so that he could preach the Good News of Christ. Help us to know You well so that we may faithfully live our lives as followers of Christ.

Patron of Notaries

MARK was converted by Peter, and accompanied him to Rome, acting as his secretary or interpreter. When Peter was writing his first epistle to the churches of Asia, he joined with his own greeting that of his faithful companion, whom he called "my son Mark."

The Roman people begged Mark to put in writing the accounts of Peter's frequent talks on our Lord's life. This the Evangelist did under the direction of Peter some time before the year 60. He wrote the second Gospel in Greek for the Gentile converts to Christianity. He is represented by a lion because his Gospel begins with St. John the Baptist, "the voice of one crying in the desert."

Mark accompanied Paul and Barnabas on their missionary journey through the island of Cyprus. Later he accompanied Barnabas alone. He was in Rome with Peter and Paul.

Mark was sent to Egypt to found the Church of Alexandria. Here he set up the first Christian school which became very famous.

One day Mark was seized by the heathen, dragged over stones, and thrown into prison. He was consoled by angels and the voice of Jesus before he went to his reward.

35

PETER was born in Holland on May 8, 1521. He attended a retreat given by Blessed Peter Faber, the first disciple of St. Ignatius, and decided to become a Jesuit. He became known for his preaching and writing. St. Ignatius kept him by his side for five months. On the day of his final vows, as he knelt in St. Peter's, he was favored with a vision of the Sacred Heart. From that time he never failed to make an offering of all his work to the Sacred Heart of Jesus.

Peter was sent to Germany where he attacked heretical teaching. He wrote a catechism which was translated into many languages. He founded a number of colleges. He also addressed the Council of Trent on the subject of the Sacrament of the Holy Eucharist.

Peter was the second great Apostle of Germany.

Peter died in Switzerland in 1597. Pope Pius XI canonized him in 1925, and proclaimed him a Doctor of the Church. He was one of the greatest opponents of the Reformation through his preaching and publication of books in defense of the Faith.

SAINT PETER CANISIUS

December 21

O God, You endowed Your Priest, St. Peter Canisius, with holiness and learning for the defense of the Church. Through his intercession, grant that those who seek the truth may joyfully find You and that the people of believers may ever persevere in bearing witness to You.

Patron of the Catholic Press

Lord, may the prayers of St. Paul who loved the Cross with a singular love gain Your grace for us. May we be inspired by his example and embrace our own cross with courage.

PAUL was born in Genoa, January 3, 1694. His youth was spent in great innocence and piety. One day in a vision he was inspired to found a congregation in honor of the Passion of Jesus Christ. He was vested by the bishop with the habit that had been shown to him in the vision, the same that the Passionists wear at the present time. He chose as the badge of his Order a heart with three nails, in memory of the sufferings of Jesus.

Paul began as a layman to preach the Passion of Christ. Many crosses tested his vocation. All his first companions, except his brother, deserted him. Finally, in 1741, the Rule he wrote was approved by Benedict XIV. The first house of the Passionists was opened at Orbitello. Later, Paul established a larger community at the Church of Sts. John and Paul in Rome.

For fifty years Paul remained the untiring missionary of Italy. God granted him marvelous gifts of soul, but he treated himself with the greatest severity, believing himself to be a useless servant and a great sinner. He died at Rome in the year 1775, at the age of eighty-one, while the Passion was being read to him.

CATHERINE was the youngest of a very large family. In 1353, at the age of six she had a vision in St. Dominic's church in which our Lord appeared to her and blessed her.

She felt that our Lord wanted her to do some special work, so she prepared for it by penance and fervent prayer.

Her parents wanted her to marry, but she put on the robes of the Sisters of the Third Order of St. Dominic and devoted herself to the care of the poor. She had many temptations, but overcame them through constant prayer. Her sound advice and wisdom were sought by civil leaders, and even by the Pope.

The Popes had been living in France instead of in Rome for many years because of the unsettled times. Catherine made a special visit to Pope Gregory XI and said, "Holy Father, God wants the head of His Church to live in Rome. I pray that you will go there as soon as possible." And once again Rome became the home of the Popes.

Catherine's last days were full of suffering, which she offered up for all Christians. Our Lord granted her a vision showing the beauty of a soul in the state of grace. She died at the age of thirty-three.

SAINT CATHERINE OF SIENA

April 29

O God, You caused St. Catherine to shine with Divine love in the contemplation of the Lord's Passion and in the service of Your Church. By her help, grant that Your people, associated in the mystery of Christ, may ever exult in the revelation of His glory. ——

Patron of Nurses

SAINT PEREGRINE

May 2

O God, You gave to St. Peregrine an angel for his companion, the Mother of God for his teacher, and Jesus for the Physician of his illness. Grant us, through his prayers, a greater love for our holy Angel, the Blessed Virgin, and our Savior.

Patron of Cancer Patients

PEREGRINE was born in 1260 at Forli, Italy. He belonged to an anti-papal party. St. Philip Benizi was sent by the Pope to preach peace at Forli. Peregrine knocked down the holy man by striking him on the face. The saint's only reply was to pray for the youth. This impressed Peregrine, and he begged forgiveness on his knees.

The Blessed Mother appeared to Peregrine and told him to go to Siena, where he was received into the Order of the Servants of Mary by St. Philip himself.

Peregrine was to have his foot cut off because of a spreading cancer. While spending the night before the operation in prayer, he fell asleep before the image of the crucified Savior. In a dream, Christ seemed to stretch out His hand from the cross and touch his diseased foot. On awakening he was completely cured.

For sixty-two years Peregrine lived a life of penance and prayer as a saintly priest. He died in 1345. He was chosen by the Church to be the patron of those suffering from running sores and cancer. Four hundred years after burial, the body of "the Cancer Saint" was found to be incorrupt.

SAINT DOMINIC SAVIO

March 9

Lord God, You alone are holy and no one is good without You. Through the intercession of St. Dominic help us to live in such a way that we may not be deprived of a share in Your glory.

Patron of Children

AMONG the boys whom St. John Bosco helped, there was one whom he loved very much—Dominic Savio. He even wrote the story of his life.

Dominic was born in Riva, Italy, in 1842. When he was five years old, he learned to serve Mass. At twelve he visited St. John Bosco and told him that he wanted to be a priest. They became good friends. Dominic entered the Oratory school, which St. John Bosco founded.

His schoolmates liked him because he was very kind and cheerful. He studied hard and loved to pray. But his health was poor, and after two years he had to return home.

Dominic always kept these rules, which he had written in a notebook on his First Communion Day: 1. I will go to Confession and to Communion often. 2. I will keep holy the Feastdays. 3. Jesus and Mary will be my best friends. 4. I will rather die than commit a sin.

When Dominic was dying, he said, "What beautiful things I see!" He was only fifteen years old.

SAINTS PHILIP AND JAMES

May 3

Lord God, we enjoy celebrating the annual feast of Your Apostles Sts. Philip and James. Through their prayers let us share in the Passion and the Resurrection of Your Son and help us merit Your eternal presence.

St. James — Patron of Hat-Makers

PHILIP was of Bethsaida. When Philip saw Christ for the first time, he went to Nathaniel and told him about the Master: "We have found Him of whom Moses in the law and the prophets wrote, Jesus of Nazareth, the Son of Joseph." Nathaniel asked, "Can any good come out of Nazareth?" Philip answered, "Come and see." Both followed our Lord.

At the Last Supper Philip said, "Lord, show us the Father and it is enough for us." He preached the Gospel in Asia Minor and was crucified there in the year 80. This is the meaning of the cross he holds.

James the Less was a cousin of our Lord and a brother of the Apostle Jude. He was known as James the Just, because from the time he was a very young man he had led a life of penance and prayer.

James was given one of the first visions of the Risen Savior. He was appointed Bishop of Jerusalem and was highly respected by Jews and Gentiles. At the age of eighty-six, he was flung from the top of a tower for honoring Christ as the Son of God. He was then struck on the head as he prayed for his enemies. The sword represents his martyrdom for Christ.

41

SAINT ROBERT BELLARMINE

September 17

O God, in order to defend the Faith You endowed St. Robert, Your Bishop, with wondrous erudition and virtues. Through his intercession, grant that Your people may ever rejoice in the integrity of that Faith.

——

Patron of Catechists

ROBERT was born in Italy in 1542. He began his novitiate in the Society of Jesus. Ill health was his cross all during his life. After his ordination, Robert became the great defender of the Church against the followers of the Protestant Reformation. Laymen and clergy, Catholics and Protestants, read his volumes with eagerness. He revised the Latin Bible as we have it today and wrote the preface for it. He was made Rector of the Jesuit College, Provincial of his Order in Naples, and theologian to Clement VIII. He wrote two famous catechisms. The Pope nominated him a cardinal because he said "he had not his equal for learning."

Having been appointed Archbishop of Capua, he laid aside his books and began preaching to the people, teaching catechism to the children, visiting the sick, and helping the poor. But three years later Pope Paul V insisted on having Cardinal Bellarmine at his side. From then on he was head of the Vatican Library. As a member of almost every Congregation, he took an important part in the affairs of the Holy See. He died at the age of seventy-nine in 1621.

JOHN La Salle was born in Rheims, France in 1651. He went to the seminary in Paris, but after the death of his parents he had to leave to look after his brothers and sisters. A few years later he returned to his studies and was ordained. He was admired for his great devotion to the Blessed Sacrament.

John was asked to help in two schools in which the teachers were trying to educate their pupils free of charge. He directed the teachers for four years, and then decided to spend his life with them. He gave away the large fortune his parents had left him. He and the young men then took vows to labor as teachers all their lives, and this was the beginning of the congregation of the Brothers of the Christian Schools, or Christian Brothers.

During his lifetime John introduced new methods of education. He divided the pupils into grades and started the first normal school to train teachers. He also started high schools and technical schools where children might learn a trade. He is often called the "father of modern education."

St. John died at Rouen in 1719. He was canonized in 1900.

SAINT JOHN BAPTIST DE LA SALLE

April 7

God our Father, You chose St. John Baptist de la Salle as an educator of Christian youth. Give Your Church good teachers today, who will dedicate themselves to instructing young people in human and Christian disciplines.

Patron of Educators

SAINT DYMPHNA

May 15

Hear us, O God, our Savior, as we honor St. Dymphna, patroness of those afflicted with mental and emotional illness. Help us to be inspired by her example and comforted by her merciful help.

Patroness of the
Mentally Ill

ST. Dymphna was born in the seventh century. Her father, Damon, a chieftain of great wealth and power, was a pagan. Her mother was a very beautiful and devout Christian.

Dymphna was fourteen when her mother died. Damon is said to have been afflicted with a mental illness, brought on by his grief. He sent messengers throughout his own and other lands to find some woman of noble birth, resembling his wife, who would be willing to marry him. When none could be found, his evil advisers told him to marry his own daughter. Dymphna fled from her castle together with St. Gerebran, her confessor, and two other friends.

Damon found them in Belgium. He gave orders that the priest's head be cut off. Then Damon tried to persuade his daughter to return to Ireland with him. When she refused, he drew his sword and struck off her head. She was then only fifteen years of age.

Dymphna received the crown of martyrdom in defense of her purity about the year 620. She is the patron of those suffering from nervous and mental afflictions. Many miracles have taken place at her shrine, built on the spot where she was buried in Gheel, Belgium.

SAINT
JOHN
NEPOMUCENE

May 16

O God, we praise You for the grace You granted to St. John to offer his life in defense of the seal of confession. Grant that, through his prayers, we may use the Sacrament of Penance often and with great profit.

Patron of Confessors

IN his early childhood, John Nepomucene was cured of a disease through the prayers of his good parents. In thanksgiving, they consecrated him to the service of God.

After he was ordained, he was sent to a parish in the city of Prague. He became a great preacher, and thousands of those who listened to him changed their way of life.

Father John was invited to the court of Wenceslaus IV. He settled arguments and did many kind deeds for the needy people of the city. He also became the queen's confessor. When the king was cruel to the queen, Father John taught her to bear her cross patiently.

One day the king asked him to tell what the queen had said in confession. When Father John refused, he was thrown into prison.

A second time, he was asked to reveal the queen's confession. "If you do not tell me," said the king, "you shall die. But if you obey my command, riches and honors will be yours." Again Father John refused. He was tortured. The king ordered him to be thrown into the river. Where he drowned, a strange brightness appeared upon the water. He is known as the "Martyr of the Confessional."

SAINT RITA

May 22

Heavenly Father, You granted to St. Rita a share in the Passion of Your Son. Give us courage and strength in time of trial, so that by our patient endurance we may enter more deeply into the Paschal Mystery of Your Son.

Patroness of Impossible Cases

AT an early age Rita begged her parents to allow her to enter a convent. Instead they arranged a marriage for her.

Rita became a good wife and mother, but her husband was a man of violent temper. In anger he often mistreated his wife. He taught their children his own evil ways. Rita tried to perform her duties faithfully and to pray and receive the sacraments frequently.

Her husband was stabbed by an enemy, but before he died he repented because Rita prayed for him.

Shortly afterwards her two sons died, and Rita was alone in the world. Prayer, fasting, penances of many kinds, and good works filled her days. She was admitted to the convent of the Augustinian nuns and began a life of perfect obedience and great charity.

Sister Rita had a great devotion to the Passion of Christ. "Please let me suffer like You, divine Savior," she said one day, and suddenly one of the thorns from the crucifix struck her on the forehead. It left a deep wound which did not heal and which caused her much suffering until her death on May 22, 1457.

SAINT MADELEINE SOPHIE BARAT

May 25

Lord Jesus Christ, after the model of Your Sacred Heart, You wonderfully graced St. Madeleine Sophie with humility and love. Make us cling always to Your most Sacred Heart and find our joy in becoming Your companions.

M ADELEINE was born in France, December 12, 1779. In Paris, she met Father Joseph Varin, who wanted to found a congregation of women devoted to the Sacred Heart and dedicated to the education of girls.

On November 21, 1800, Madeleine Sophie and three other postulants began their religious life. The following year she was sent to Amiens to teach in a school; this was the first convent of the new Order. Soon a second school—a free one for poor children—was opened. Though she was only twenty-three, Madeleine Sophie was appointed superior and held that office for sixty-three years. As Superior General of the Society of the Sacred Heart, she built one hundred and five houses in the principal countries of the world, including the United States.

Madeleine Sophie exhorted her religious at all times to seek the glory of the Heart of Jesus in laboring for the sanctification of souls. Her motto was: "To suffer myself and not to make others suffer."

She died at Paris, May 25, 1865, and was canonized May 24, 1925.

PHILIP was born in Florence in 1515. His family was poor. Philip went to Rome to act as teacher for two boys. He began to visit the hospitals of the city, taking a great interest in the sick and in poor pilgrims, and it was not long before he had formed a society for this work.

After he was ordained priest, Philip stayed with his society. He helped the boys of Rome when they were in trouble. He found places for them to play. He would help a poor man, nurse a sick man, look for money for a poor pilgrim, or console a sinner in the confessional.

Philip encouraged frequent confession and Communion. He was not strict with people, but he expected them to do their best. Young and old, attracted by his cheerful holiness, came in large numbers to hear his words of wisdom. In order to spread his work, he founded the Congregation of the Oratory, a group of priests dedicated to preaching and teaching.

For sixty-two years Philip gave wise advice and a holy example to all classes of people in Rome and filled their hearts with love of God. In the year 1595 he passed away quietly.

SAINT PHILIP NERI

May 26

O God, You never cease raising Your faithful servants to the glory of holiness. Grant that we may be inflamed by the fire of the Holy Spirit which so wonderfully burned in the heart of St. Philip.

———

Patron of Rome

SAINT JOAN OF ARC

May 30

O Lord, You raised up in a wondrous manner St. Joan, Your Virgin, to defend the Faith and her country. Grant that through her prayers Your Church may enjoy lasting peace.

Patroness of France and Soldiers

JOAN was born in France in 1412. She helped her brothers on the farm and often went to a nearby chapel to pray to Jesus.

When she was seventeen, Joan heard the voice of God calling her to drive the enemies of France from the land. Going to the king, whose army had been defeated, she asked for a small army. The king, believing that God had sent her to save France, gave her a band of brave soldiers. Joan had a great love for Jesus whom she often received in Holy Communion. She also had a devotion to the angels, especially St. Michael.

Joan went before the soldiers carrying her banner with the words: "Jesus, Mary." The soldiers became filled with courage and drove the British army into retreat. Charles VII was crowned king of France.

Later, Joan fell into the hands of the British and remained in chains for nine months. Then she was taken to the marketplace of Rouen and burned to death. With her eyes on a crucifix, she cried out, "Jesus, Jesus," through the flames.

SAINT ANGELA MERICI

January 27

O Lord, let St. Angela never cease commending us to Your kindness. By always imitating her charity and prudence may we succeed in keeping Your teachings and reflecting them in our lives.

ANGELA was born in Italy in the year 1470. At fifteen years of age she became a tertiary of St. Francis. In a vision God revealed to her that she would inspire a group of devout women to give themselves to the service of God.

When she was about twenty-two, Angela returned to her home town to find that parents were not teaching their children the simplest truths of religion. She talked the matter over with her friends. They gathered together the little girls of the neighborhood to whom they gave regular instruction. Angela began with twelve companions at Brescia. This was the beginning of the Ursuline Order—the first teaching Order of women to be founded in the Church. As a patron, Angela chose St. Ursula because, ever since her martyrdom, this saint was regarded as the ideal example of Christian virginity.

In 1535, twenty-eight young women consecrated themselves with her to the service of God. These women lived a holy life in the midst of their families. They met together for classes and spiritual exercises, and carried out the duties given to them. Angela was chosen their superior, and continued to fill that office for the last five years of her life.

SAINT BONIFACE

June 5

O Lord, let St. Boniface intercede for us, that we may firmly adhere to the Faith he taught, and for which he shed his blood, and fearlessly profess it in our works.

Patron of Germany

BONIFACE was born in 680 in Devonshire, England. From the age of thirteen he was educated in the Benedictine monastery of Exeter, where he later became a monk.

He went to Rome to obtain the Pope's blessing on his mission to the German people. It was a slow and dangerous task. He destroyed the temples of idols and built churches on their site. Once he cut down a huge oak which was dedicated to the god Jupiter, and then used the tree in building a church dedicated to St. Peter.

Boniface was recalled to Rome, consecrated bishop by the Pope, and returned to extend and organize the Church in Germany. In 745, he chose Mainz as his Episcopal See, after he had established a number of dioceses. He corrected abuses and built religious houses.

Boniface set out to convert a pagan tribe in Holland. While he was waiting to administer Confirmation to some newly-baptized Christians, a troop of pagans arrived. His attendants would have opposed them, but he said, "My children, do not resist." The pagans killed the saint and fifty-two Christians who were with him on June 5, 755. St. Boniface is the patron saint of Germany.

SAINT ANTHONY OF PADUA

June 13

Almighty, ever-living God, You gave Your people the extraordinary preacher St. Anthony and made him an intercessor in difficulties. By his aid grant that we may live a truly Christian life and experience Your help in all adversities.

Patron of the Poor

ANTHONY'S parents were very rich and wanted him to be a great nobleman. But he wanted to be poor for the sake of Jesus Christ, so he became a Franciscan.

Anthony was a great preacher. He was sent out as a missionary and preached in many cities in Italy and France. He brought many sinners back to God mostly by his good example.

One day, when Anthony was praying in his room, the Infant Jesus appeared to him, put His little arms around his neck, and kissed him. This wonderful favor was given to him because he kept his soul free from even the smallest sin and because he loved Jesus very much.

When he became ill he went to a monastery outside of Padua, where he prepared for death.

Many miracles took place after his death on June 13, 1231. Even today he is called the "wonder-worker." He was only thirty-six years old when he died. Thirty-two years after his death his remains were brought to Padua. The flesh was all consumed except the tongue, which was found red and fresh as it was while he was living.

SAINT BASIL THE GREAT

January 2

Hear our prayer, O Lord, which we offer in honor of St. Basil, Your Bishop. By his merits and prayers may we be found worthy to serve You well and be absolved from all our sins.

Patron of Hospital Administrators

BASIL was born at Caesarea, in Asia Minor, in the year 329. His father and mother were nobles and also saints. There were ten children in the family, four of whom became canonized saints.

Basil went to school in Constantinople and then in Athens where he lived with his friend, St. Gregory Nazianzen. The two friends became great scholars. Basil opened a school of oratory and practiced law in Caesarea. So many people wished to hear him speak in public that he was tempted by thoughts of pride. He therefore sold all his goods, gave the money to the poor, and became a monk. He consecrated to God all his knowledge and eloquence.

Basil visited the monks who lived in the desert. He then founded several monasteries and drew up rules for the monks. Although Basil was in poor health, he performed many penances.

Basil became the Archbishop of Caesarea and defended the freedom of his people against the Roman Emperor.

Basil wrote many books and defended the Church against the Arian heretics. He was given the title "Doctor of the Church," and "Father of the Church." He died in 379.

SAINT ALOYSIUS GONZAGA

June 21

O God, the Giver of heavenly gifts, You united a wonderful innocence of life with a spirit of penance in the angelic youth, Aloysius. Grant through his prayers that we may imitate him in his penance.

———

Patron of Youth

ALOYSIUS lived in the castle of the Gonzaga family. As a little boy he spent some time with his father in the army. There he picked up rough language. His mother scolded him and taught him what a terrible thing it is to offend God even in a small matter. He began to love prayer and to think very seriously about his soul.

Aloysius was sent to Madrid, in Spain, to become a page to a prince, and to receive an education. But his motto was: "I was born for greater things." At twenty he signed away forever his right to the title and lands of the Gonzagas and became a Jesuit novice. His fellow students loved him because he was kind and willing to help them. They respected him because of his great love for purity.

In Rome he nursed the victims of disease in a hospital, and before long he himself was ill. The sores caused by the disease were very painful. Aloysius never reached the priesthood. On June 21, 1591, he passed away quietly as he gazed at a crucifix where he found strength to suffer. He was only twenty-three years old.

JOHN was the son of the priest Zachary. His birth was foretold by the Angel Gabriel during a vision to Zachary in the Temple. John lived in the desert for years. He ate only locusts and wild honey, and never touched strong drink. He wore a rough garment of camel's skin. His hair reached his shoulders.

At the River Jordan John cried out: "Do penance, for the kingdom of heaven is at hand! I am the voice of one crying in the wilderness. Make straight the way of the Lord." Large crowds were baptized by him as a sign of penance.

John pointed to Jesus with the words, "Behold the Lamb of God who takes away the sins of the world!" And when John poured water over the head of Jesus as a sign of penance, the Holy Spirit appeared in the form of a dove, and the Heavenly Father said, "This is My Beloved Son, in whom I am well pleased."

When John warned King Herod that it was not lawful for him to have his brother's wife, he was thrown into prison. Later the king had him beheaded. Our Lord said of John: "Among those that are born of women, there is not a greater prophet than John the Baptist."

SAINT JOHN THE BAPTIST

June 24

O God, You raised up St. John the Baptist to prepare a perfect people for Christ. Fill Your people with the joy of possessing Your grace and direct the minds of of all the faithful in the way of peace and salvation.

SAINT PETER THE APOSTLE

June 29

O God, You were glorified by the martyrdom of Your Apostle, St. Peter. Grant that Your Church may in all things follow the teaching of him whom the Savior made the Head of His Church.

SIMON was a fisherman. His brother Andrew said to him, "I have met Jesus. Come and see Him." Simon loved Jesus and Jesus gave him the name Peter, which means "a rock."

Jesus picked eleven other Apostles and said to them, "Follow Me, and I will make you fishers of men." He meant that He would send them to do His work of bringing people to God. The Apostles gave up their homes to follow Jesus.

One day Jesus said to them, "Who do you think I am?" Peter answered, "You are Christ, the Son of God."

Our Lord was pleased and said, "You are Peter, a rock, and I will build My church upon you. I will give you the keys of the kingdom of heaven." This is the power to help people get to heaven.

After His Resurrection, Jesus asked Peter three times, "Peter, do you love Me?" Three times Peter answered, "Lord, You know that I love You." And Jesus said to him, "Feed My lambs, feed My sheep." In this way Jesus made it clear that Peter was to be the first pope.

Peter was crucified, head downward, in Rome, because he said he was not worthy to die the same way as Jesus.

SAINT PAUL THE APOSTLE

June 29

O God, by the preaching of St. Paul, the Apostle, You taught the multitude of the Gentiles. Grant that we who venerate his example may also share in his prayers.

SAUL was a Jew who hated the Christians. He was on his way to the city of Damascus to arrest them when a light from heaven suddenly shone around him. He fell to the ground as he heard a voice saying, "Saul, Saul, why do you persecute Me?"

He asked, "Who are You, Lord?" And the voice answered, "I am Jesus, whom you are persecuting." Saul asked, "Lord, what do You want me to do?" The voice said, "Go into the city; you will be told what to do."

Saul had to be led by his companions into the city, as he had been struck blind. After three days, a man named Ananias came to him and said, "Brother Saul, the Lord has sent me—Jesus who appeared to you on your journey—that you may get your sight back and be filled with the Holy Spirit."

At once Saul could see. He was baptized and was called Paul. He began to preach the word of Jesus to the pagan world. (The picture shows him in Athens.) He wrote many letters (epistles) to the Christians.

After years of travel and suffering, Paul was taken to Rome as a prisoner and beheaded.

MARIA was a beautiful Italian girl of twelve who lived on a farm. One day Alessandro, a nineteen-year-old boy, was helping on the farm. He stopped at Maria's house and wanted to do wrong with her.

"No! No!" Maria cried out. "Do not touch me, Alessandro! It is a sin. You will go to hell!"

When Maria began to fight him, he took a knife and stabbed her fourteen times. Maria fell to the floor with a cry of pain, "O God, I am dying! Mamma! Mamma!" Alessandro ran out of the room.

Maria was taken to the hospital and suffered there for two days. When the priest asked her if she would forgive her murderer, she said, "Yes, I forgive him for the love of Jesus . . . and I want him to be with me in heaven. May God forgive him!"

Maria died kissing the crucifix and holding a medal of Our Lady. This happened in 1902.

Maria Goretti was canonized by Pope Pius XII in 1950. She was chosen to be the patron of boys and girls, that she might help them to be pure.

SAINT MARIA GORETTI

July 6

O God, Author of innocence and Lover of chastity, You conferred on St. Maria Your handmaid the grace of martyrdom at a youthful age. Through her intercession grant us constancy in Your commandments, You Who gave the crown to a virgin who fought for You.

Patroness of Children
of Mary

SAINTS CYRIL AND METHODIUS

February 14

Merciful God, You have enlightened the Slavonic nations by the teaching of the brothers Cyril and Methodius. Help us to assimilate the teachings of Your doctrine and perfect us as a people united in the true Faith and its expansion.

Patrons of Moravia

THE two brothers, Cyril and Methodius, belonged to a senatorial family of Thessalonica, but their mother was probably a Slav. Cyril went to Constantinople, where he was ordained priest. He taught philosophy in the university and defended the Gospel of Christ. The older brother, Methodius, after being governor of one of the Slav colonies, became the abbot of a monastery in Greece.

In 862, Ratislav, the Prince of Moravia, asked the Emperor, Michael III, to send him Christian missionaries to teach his people in their own language. The two brothers were sent to the court of Ratislav at Velehrad. They needed bishops to ordain more priests. They journeyed to Rome bringing with them the relics of Pope St. Clement. Pope Adrian II consecrated them bishops and approved the use of the Liturgy in the Slavonic tongue.

Cyril died in Rome. Methodius continued the apostolate with success in Moravia, Bohemia, Poland and the neighboring countries. He introduced the Slav alphabet and translated the Holy Scriptures into the Slavonic language. He died in Moravia, April 6, 885. Sts. Cyril and Methodius are honored as the apostles of the Slavs.

SAINT THOMAS MORE

June 22

O God, You willed that the witness of martyrdom should be the finest expression of the Faith. Through the intercession of St. Thomas, grant that we may confirm by the testimony of our lives that Faith which we profess with our tongues.

———

Patron of Lawyers

THOMAS More went to school in London. He served as a page for the Archbishop of Canterbury. Later, he studied law.

Thomas married, and he and his family lived happily, sharing their means with the poor. After the death of his wife, Thomas remarried for the sake of his four children.

King Henry VIII made him Chancellor of England, a position second only to that of the king himself. Thomas enforced the laws of England and saw that the poor were protected against injustice.

Once while Thomas was hearing Mass, King Henry sent for him. He did not leave until the Mass was finished, but sent this message: "As soon as my audience with the King of Heaven is ended, I will at once obey the desire of my earthly king."

King Henry wanted a law passed making himself head of the Church of England, because the Pope would not grant him a divorce from the Queen. When Thomas refused to consider such a law and resigned his position, he was arrested. At the trial false witnesses were called against him, and he was condemned to death. He prayed for the king before he was beheaded.

BONAVENTURE was born in Tuscany, Italy, in 1221. His mother begged St. Francis to pray for the recovery of her son from a dangerous illness. Foreseeing the future greatness of this child, Francis cried out, "O buona ventura!—O good fortune!"

At the age of twenty-two, Bonaventure entered the Franciscan Order. He was sent to Paris to complete his studies under great scholars. There he became the close friend of St. Thomas Aquinas, and with him received the degree of Doctor of Theology. He also enjoyed the friendship of King St. Louis.

St. Thomas asked Bonaventure one day where he acquired his great learning. He replied by pointing to his crucifix. At another time Thomas found him writing the life of St. Francis, and exclaimed, "Let us leave a saint to write of a saint!"

At the age of thirty-five he was made general of his Order. Later Pope Gregory X appointed him a cardinal. He spoke first at the Council of Lyons. He died in 1274.

St. Bonaventure is known as the "Seraphic Doctor," from the warmth of divine love which is found in his writings.

SAINT BONAVEN-TURE

July 15

Almighty God, today we celebrate the heavenly birthday of St. Bonaventure, Your Bishop. Let us benefit by his wonderful teaching and always be inspired by his burning charity.

SAINT CAMILLUS OF LELLIS

July 14

O God, You adorned St. Camillus, Your Priest, with the singular grace of charity toward the sick. By his merits, pour forth the spirit of Your love into us, so that by serving You in our brothers here on earth we may safely come to You at the hour of death.

———

Patron of Hospitals

CAMILLUS was born in Italy in 1550. In his youth he became a soldier and led a wayward life. He lost so much in gambling that he was forced to work as a laborer on a building belonging to the Capuchins, where he was converted. Three times he entered the Capuchin novitiate, but each time a wound in his leg forced him to leave. He went to Rome for medical treatment, and there took St. Philip Neri as his confessor.

Camillus entered the hospital for incurables; some time later he had charge of it. At the age of thirty-two, he began to study grammar with children. He was ordained priest, and in 1586 his Congregation of the Servants of the Sick was approved by the Pope.

The Brothers served the sick not only in hospitals but also in their homes. They were inspired by the example of Camillus who, day and night, served the patients, consoled them, and prayed with them. He honored the sick as living images of Christ, and by serving them in this spirit he did penance for the sins of his youth. He received his inspiration and strength from the crucifix. He died in 1614.

SAINT VINCENT DE PAUL

September 27

O God, You gave St. Vincent de Paul apostolic virtues for the salvation of the poor and the formation of the clergy. Grant that, endowed with the same spirit, we may love what he loved and act according to his teaching.

Patron of Charitable Societies

VINCENT was born in France in 1581. When he was still a young priest, he was captured by Turkish pirates who sold him into slavery. For two years he had to work hard for the masters who bought him. He converted his last master and was then set free.

Vincent was sent to do parish work near Paris. He was a very great friend of the poor. He organized groups to look after the needy. The women nursed the sick and cooked meals for them. Men found jobs for the poor who were able to work, and gave food and clothes to those who could not work. Vincent also founded the Daughters of Charity. With the help of these Sisters he gathered money to clothe and feed the poor and to nurse the sick. He built homes for the poor, for the sick, for the aged, and for abandoned children.

Vincent also founded the Congregation of the Mission, or Lazarists, a society of priests and missionaries.

He was almost eighty years old when he died in Paris, in 1660. His body was found to be incorrupt fifty years after his death.

St. Vincent is called the Apostle of Organized Charity. The St. Vincent de Paul Society continues his work for the poor.

SAINT MARY MAGDALEN

July 22

O God, it was to St. Mary Magdalen before all others that Your Son committed the message of Easter joy. Through her intercession may we proclaim Christ as our living Lord and one day contemplate Him reigning in glory.

MARY of Magdala was known to all as "The Sinner." Filled with deep sorrow because of her sinful life, she went to a dinner to which Jesus was invited. She washed His feet with her tears, wiped them with her hair, and poured rich perfume upon them.

Simon, who invited Jesus, was thinking: "If this man were a prophet He would know who this woman is."

Jesus said to him, "I came into your house and you did not give Me water to wash My feet, but this woman washed My feet with her tears and wiped them with her hair. Her many sins are forgiven because she has loved Me very much."

Then Jesus said to Mary, "Your sins are forgiven. Your faith has saved you. Go in peace."

Because Mary Magdalen was thankful, she followed Jesus everywhere and helped Him in His needs. She stood at the foot of the Cross with the Mother of Jesus. After His Resurrection, our Lord appeared to her and said, "Mary," and she answered, "My Master!"

Mary Magdalen spent the rest of her life doing penance for her sins. The skull and cross mean death and sacrifice.

JAMES was the son of Zebedee and Salome. His younger brother was John the Evangelist. He is called "the greater" because he was called to be an Apostle before the other Apostle James.

When John the Baptist pointed out Christ on the Jordan, James followed his brother John to the Messias and began his life of devotion and love. He was with Jesus at the wedding feast of Cana. When Jesus told the disciples that He would make them "fishers of men," James left his nets and everything else to follow our Lord.

On the day of the Transfiguration, Peter, James and John were present. Our Lord took them with Him into the Garden of Olives.

Jesus called James a "son of thunder" because of the flaming, great love of his soul for the Master.

James preached the Gospel in Samaria and Judea. He also made a journey to Spain, and is honored as the patron saint of that country. He was the first of the Apostles to give his life for Christ, having been killed with the sword by King Herod Agrippa in the year 43.

SAINT JAMES THE GREATER

July 25

Almighty and ever-living God, through the blood of St. James You consecrated the first fruits of the ministry of Your Apostles. Grant that Your Church may be strengthened by his confession and always enjoy his patronage.

———

Patron of Laborers

SAINT CHRISTOPHER

July 25

Almighty and ever-living God, graciously pour out Your Spirit upon us. Let our hearts be filled with that true love which enabled Your holy Martyr Christopher to overcome all bodily torments.

———

Patron of Motorists

A big man of giant strength, whose name was Offero, lived in the land of Chanaan many years ago. Looking for adventure, he left his native land saying, "I will roam through the whole world in search of the mightiest of kings, and be his servant."

He came at last upon a hermit who guarded a dangerous passage across a stream, and guided travelers to a place where they could cross with safety. This man of God instructed the giant about our Lord, the greatest King. Offero settled down near the stream and carried travelers across on his shoulders to serve the great King.

One day he carried a little boy on his shoulders. The water began to rise while the boy on his shoulders grew heavier. Offero cried out, "Child, how heavy you are! I feel as if I were carrying the whole world upon my shoulders."

The little boy answered smiling, "You are carrying more than the world; you are carrying Him who created heaven and earth."

Saying these words, the boy dipped His hand into the water and baptized Offero. Since then he is called Christopher or Christ-bearer.

St. Christopher died a martyr.

SAINT ANNE

July 26

O God, You bestowed on St. Anne such grace that she was found worthy to become the mother of Mary, who brought forth Your Only-begotten Son. Grant that we may be helped by her intercession.

———

Patron of Housewives

S T. ANNE was the mother of the Blessed Virgin and the grandmother of Jesus Christ.

She and her husband were rich, and very devoted to God. Their home was Nazareth. They had no children, and that was believed to be a punishment of God among the Jews. For this reason Joachim would not even offer sacrifice in the temple. He was very sad and went into the mountains to pray. Anne prayed to God in her home and begged Him to give her a child. She promised to dedicate her child to His service.

Their prayers were heard. An angel came to Anne and said, "Anne, the Lord has looked upon your tears. You will give birth to a daughter, and she will be honored by all the world." The angel made the same promise to Joachim.

A daughter was born to Anne, and she called her Miriam, which means "Mary." Anne offered her child to God in the service of the temple at a very early age.

St. Anne's name means "grace." God endowed her with special gifts and graces to be the mother of the Mother of God.

SAINT IGNATIUS LOYOLA

July 31

O God, You raised up St. Ignatius in Your Church to inspire men to work for Your greater glory. Grant that we may labor on earth with his help and after his example and merit to be crowned with him in heaven.

———

Patron of Retreats

IGNATIUS of Loyola was a soldier. His leg was badly broken. Three times he had it set, even though he suffered great pain, because he wanted to march and dance again.

As he lay ill in a castle, he picked up a book on the Lives of the Saints and started to read. He became interested and wondered if he could do what the saints had done.

When he left the castle, he went to confession. For almost a year he lived in a cave on the banks of a river. Here he punished himself for his sins. He fasted, prayed and took care of the poor and the sick.

In Barcelona, Spain, he entered school—a man thirty-five years old. At Paris he formed, with his first five followers, the Society of Jesus. This was the beginning of the Jesuit Order. Schools, preaching, retreats, missionary work—any work was to be their work, especially at a time when many were falling away from the Church. Even in America his men began teaching the Faith to the Indians. They would do whatever the Holy Father wished.

For fifteen years Ignatius directed the work of his Society. Almost totally blind, he died at the age of sixty-five on July 31, 1556.

SAINT ALPHONSUS LIGUORI

August 1

O God, You constantly introduce new examples of virtue in Your Church. Walking in the footsteps of St. Alphonsus Your Bishop, may we be consumed with zeal for souls and attain the rewards he has won in heaven.

———

Patron of Confessors and Moral Theologians

ALPHONSUS was born near Naples in Italy, in 1696, of a noble Italian family. At nineteen he began to practice law and became one of the leading lawyers in Naples. He never went to the law courts without having first attended Mass. He then made up his mind to become a priest. He was almost thirty years of age when he was ordained.

Alphonsus preached missions. Large crowds came to hear him. He often visited the sick. He wrote several books.

Alphonsus organized a community of priests in honor of the Most Holy Redeemer. Today the Redemptorists preach parish missions.

The Pope commanded Alphonsus to become a bishop. During the thirteen years that he was bishop, his health was never good. An attack of rheumatism left him a cripple for the rest of his life. His head was so badly bent that his chin pressed against his chest. Alphonsus was permitted to leave his diocese. He continued to preach missions and to write books. He made a vow never to waste even a moment of his time, and kept it for his entire ninety-one years.

Alphonsus had a great love for the Blessed Sacrament and Our Lady. He was given the title of "Doctor of the Church."

SAINT DOMINIC

August 8

O God, let St. Dominic help Your Church by his merits and teaching. May he who was an outstanding preacher of truth become a most generous intercessor for us.

Patron of Astronomers

DOMINIC was born in Spain of a wealthy family. Some years after his ordination, the bishop took Dominic with him on a visit to southern France where a heresy, or doctrine opposed to the teachings of the Church, was being taught. Many people were leaving the Church to follow this false teaching. Dominic decided to remain in France and devote his life to preaching and to leading people back to the Faith. The dog carrying a torch represents the fire of his zeal for souls.

He went to Rome and told the Pope that he wanted to establish a religious order whose duties would be preaching and teaching. The new order was called the Order of Preachers, or the Dominicans.

Once when Dominic became discouraged with the slow progress of his work, Our Lady appeared to him with a beautiful wreath of roses. She asked him to say the rosary every day and to teach the people to say the rosary. Soon the heresy began to disappear.

Before his death in 1221, Dominic also founded an order of nuns to care for young girls.

SAINT JOHN MARY VIANNEY

August 4

Almighty and merciful God, in St. John Vianney You have given us a Priest who was outstanding in pastoral zeal. Through his intercession help us to win others for Christ and together with them attain eternal glory.

Patron of Priests

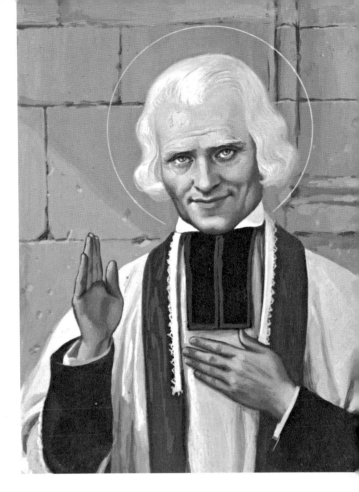

JOHN was born in France in 1786. As a boy he worked in his father's fields. After work, he taught other children their prayers and catechism.

John was slow to learn, but a parish priest helped him to enter the seminary. After years of hard study, he became a priest.

Father Vianney was sent to the little parish of Ars. The people did not come to his church, so he began to visit them in their homes.

He ate very little and lived like the poorest of the poor. He did penance for his people and prayed for hours before the Blessed Sacrament. "That is the way to win souls to God," he said. He was often tormented by the devil who tried to keep him from saving souls.

Thousands came to hear him speak and to confess their sins to him. He often spent eighteen hours a day in the confessional.

Father Vianney spent forty years as the parish priest of Ars, dying at the age of seventy-three.

St. John is the patron saint of parish priests.

SAINT LAWRENCE

August 10

O God, by his ardent love for You St. Lawrence exhibited faithful service and attained a glorious martyrdom. Help us to love what he loved and to practice what he taught.

——

Patron of Seminarians

L AWRENCE was the first of the seven deacons who served the Roman Church. His duty was to assist the Pope when celebrating Holy Mass and to give Holy Communion to the people. He was also in charge of the Church property, distributing among the poor the offerings given by the Christians.

When Pope Sixtus was led out to die, Lawrence wept that he, too, could not die along with him.

The Holy Pope said, "Do not cry, my son; in three days you will follow me."

Lawrence was arrested. When the prefect or governor of the city ordered Lawrence to turn over the treasures of the Church, he gathered the poor and the sick. Showing them to the prefect, he said, "These are the real treasures of the Church."

Lawrence was placed on a gridiron to be roasted over a slow fire. Later he said, "You may turn my body over; it is roasted enough on that side." Lawrence died in the year 258.

C LARE was the daughter of a count and countess. She heard St. Francis preach in the streets of Assisi and told him of her desire to give herself to God. They became close friends.

On Palm Sunday, in the year 1212, the Bishop of Assisi presented a palm to this noble maiden of eighteen, who was beautifully dressed. That same night she left her castle with one companion and went to the church of Our Lady of the Angels, where she met Francis and his Brothers. At the altar of Our Lady, Francis cut off her hair and Clare gave her life to Christ.

In an old house outside Assisi she started her Order of the Poor Clares. Later, her sister and mother and other noble ladies joined her. They lived a life of prayer, silence, and fasting.

One day enemies of the Church were about to attack the convent. The saint had the Blessed Sacrament placed in a monstrance above the gate of the convent and, kneeling before it, she prayed for help. Suddenly the enemy fled.

During her illness of twenty-eight years, the Holy Eucharist was her strength. She died in 1253.

SAINT CLARE

August 11

O God, in Your mercy You led St. Clare to embrace poverty. Through her intercession help us to follow Christ in the spirit of poverty and to contemplate You in the heavenly Kingdom.

Patroness of Television

73

SAINT JOHN BERCHMANS

November 26

O God, You inspired St. John Berchmans to strive for perfect charity and so attain Your Kingdom at the end his pilgrimage on earth. Strengthen us through his intercession that we may advance rejoicing in the way of love.

Patron of Altar Boys

JOHN was born at Diest, a small town in Belgium, in 1599. Of the five children in his family, three entered the religious state. As a boy John had a very great devotion to Holy Mass and the rosary.

When John was but nine years of age, his mother became ill. As many hours of each day as could be spared from school and other duties, he devoted to helping his suffering mother. For three years he was a pupil of a pastor of a parish who prepared boys for the priesthood. He entered the Jesuit novitiate in Mechlin and later traveled to Rome on foot to continue his studies.

After studying philosophy for three years, he was selected by his superiors to take part in a public debate. Before the debate was ended, he became ill. During the evening of August 12th, 1621, he clasped his rosary, his crucifix and the book of rules, and said, "These are my three treasures; with these I shall gladly die." On August 13 he passed away, his eyes still fixed upon his "treasures."

In 1888, Pope Leo XIII canonized him.

SAINT TARCISIUS

August 15

God of power and mercy, through Your help St. Tarcisius has overcome the tortures of his passion. Help us who celebrate his triumph to remain victorious over the wiles of our enemies.

Patron of
First Communicants

AT Rome, on the Appian Way, the pagans met Tarcisius, the acolyte, bearing the sacrament of the Body of Christ and asked him what it was that he carried. When he refused to give up the Sacred Host, he was attacked for a long time with sticks and stones until he died. When they turned over his body, the wicked men could find no trace of the Blessed Sacrament. The Christians buried the body of the martyr with honor in the cemetery of St. Callistus. This happened in the third or fourth century.

Pope St. Damasus wrote a poem in the fourth century in which he stated that Tarcisius, like another St. Stephen stoned by the Jews, suffered a violent death at the hands of a mob rather than give up "the divine Body of the Savior to raging dogs." For this reason Tarcisius is known as the boy martyr of the Holy Eucharist.

Probably his body rested with those of Pope St. Zephyrinus and others in the basilica of St. Sixtus and St. Cecilia, but his relics are claimed by the church of St. Sylvester.

We should ask St. Tarcisius for a greater love of Jesus in Holy Communion.

SAINT JOACHIM

July 26

O God, of all Your saints You willed St. Joachim to be father to the Mother of Your Son. Grant that we who venerate him may evermore experience his patronage.

Patron of Fathers

JOACHIM, husband of St. Anne and father of the Blessed Virgin Mary, belonged to the tribe of Juda and the House of David. He and his wife came from Galilee. They lived in Nazareth and there the Blessed Mother was born and reared.

Joachim was very sad because he and his wife did not have children. Both prayed earnestly for a child. Joachim even spent forty days and nights in the desert fasting and praying. An angel appeared to Anne and told her that she would become a mother. The angel also appeared to Joachim. He went to the temple rejoicing and offered animals to God as a sacrifice.

Joachim's greatest honor is the fact that he is the father of Mary, the Mother of God. A church was built in the fourth century, possibly by St. Helen, on the site of the home of Joachim and Anne in Jerusalem, where they were buried.

St. Joachim is a patron for good fathers.

SAINT HELEN

August 18

Lord Jesus Christ, You revealed Your Cross to St. Helen because You wanted to give us a great treasure. Grant, through her prayers, that the ransom paid on that life-giving wood may win us the rewards of everlasting life.

HELEN was a British princess. She became a Christian late in life. Her faith and piety had a good influence on her son Constantine, the first Christian Emperor. She used her wealth for charity and in building churches. When the Emperor planned to build a church on Mount Calvary, Helen, at the age of eighty, began a journey to Jerusalem, hoping to find the Holy Cross.

After many labors, three crosses were found on Mount Calvary, together with the nails and the inscriptions. The three crosses were brought before a woman who was afflicted with an incurable disease. When the third cross touched her, she was perfectly cured. With great joy the pious Empress went about building a glorious church on Mount Calvary in which she placed the precious relic of the true Cross. She sent pieces of it to Rome and Constantinople. She also had a church built on Mount Olivet.

In the year 312 Constantine obtained a great victory through the power of the Cross. Shortly after, Helen returned to Rome where she died in the year 328.

SAINT JOHN EUDES

August 19

O God, You wonderfully chose St. John, Your Priest, to announce the unsearchable riches of Christ. Help us to grow in the knowledge of You through his example and counsels and so to live faithfully according to the light of the Gospel.

JOHN EUDES was born in France, November 14, 1601. As a priest he was full of zeal for the salvation of souls. During a plague in Normandy, John spent two months ministering to the sick and dying. For the following ten years he was engaged chiefly in giving missions among the people. A bishop said of him, "I have heard all the best preachers in Italy and France, but I have never heard anyone who touches the heart so deeply as does this good Father."

His great work consisted in establishing seminaries. He founded the Congregation of Jesus and Mary to form a virtuous parochial clergy in seminaries. They wore a badge on which were inscribed the hearts of Jesus and Mary, and were not bound by vows. They were also called Eudists.

John also founded the Sisters of Our Lady of Charity to labor for the welfare of penitent women. He wrote a famous book entitled *The Devotion to the Adorable Heart of Jesus.* Pope Leo XIII recognized him as the author of the liturgical devotion to the Sacred Hearts of Jesus and Mary.

BERNARD was born in a castle in Burgundy, France. At an early age he was sent to the best schools. He studied theology and Holy Scripture. After his mother's death, fearing the temptations of the world, he made up his mind to become a monk of the Cistercian Order. His superior sent him with twelve monks to found a new monastery called the Abbey of Clairvaux. Bernard was at once appointed abbot. Every day Bernard asked himself this question: "Why have I come here?" He never allowed himself to forget that his main duty in this world was to lead a holy life and to save his soul.

The poor and the weak sought Bernard's protection; bishops, kings, and popes asked his advice. Pope Eugenius commanded him to preach a crusade through France and Germany.

Bernard founded many monasteries. He is known for his writings which have earned him the title of "the Last of the Fathers and Doctor of Holy Church." He was devoted to the Blessed Virgin and composed the beautiful prayer called "The Memorare." Bernard died in the year 1153. His greatest devotion was to Jesus Crucified to whom he dedicated all his love.

SAINT BERNARD

August 20

O God, You blessed Your Church with St. Bernard, a man full of zeal for Your house, radiating brightness and ardent love. Through his intercession, grant that we may be animated by the same spirit and always walk as children of light.

Patron of Candle-Makers

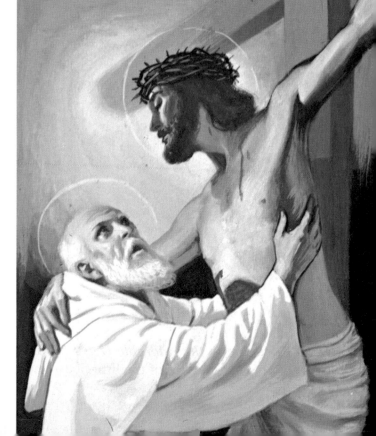

SAINT JANE FRANCES DE CHANTAL

December 12

O God, You endowed St. Jane Frances with admirable qualities in various walks of life. Through her intercession help us to be true to our vocation and never fail to bear witness to the light You give us.

JANE was the second child of the president of the French Parliament of Burgundy. At the age of twenty she married the Baron de Chantal, an officer in the army of Henry IV. Her husband was killed by accident while hunting and died in her arms. She was left a widow at the age of twenty-eight with one little son and three daughters.

Jane placed herself under the direction of St. Francis de Sales, who advised her to spend her life in the service of God. She provided well for her children. With the help of St. Francis she laid the foundation of her new "Order of the Visitation of Our Lady" at Annecy in 1610. This convent was to be a haven for those whose health, age, or other circumstances prevented them from being accepted in other orders.

St. Vincent de Paul said of her: "She was full of faith, and yet all her life long she had been tormented by thoughts against it. Nor did she once relax in the fidelity God asked of her. And so I regard her as one of the holiest souls I have ever met on this earth."

Jane visited eighty-seven convents of the Order. She died December 13, 1641, at the age of sixty-nine.

SAINT BARTHOLOMEW

August 24

Lord, strengthen in us that Faith by which Your Apostle St. Bartholomew adhered to Your Son with sincerity of mind. Through his intercession, grant that Your Church may become a sacrament of salvation for all nations.

Patron of Plasterers

BARTHOLOMEW lived near Bethsaida and was also known as Nathaniel. Philip, his friend, was a disciple of John the Baptist. One evening Philip told Nathaniel that John the Baptist had pointed out the Messias as the Redeemer and the Lamb of God who takes away the sins of the world.

When Jesus saw the two friends coming, He spoke to Nathaniel, "Behold an Israelite indeed in whom there is no evil." Nathaniel then made this act of faith: "Master, You are the Son of God. You are the King of Israel."

To be so pure and noble that even the Lord considered him "without evil" is the great honor of Nathaniel. He was honest and simple and strong in his faith.

Nathaniel was on the lake shore when Jesus showed Himself after His Resurrection. He and some of the Apostles fished all night and caught nothing. Jesus told them to cast the net once more, and they caught many fish. After the Ascension, Nathaniel preached the Gospel in Arabia and India. He suffered martyrdom in Armenia. His skin was cut from his living body.

SAINT AUGUSTINE

August 28

Lord, renew in Your Church the spirit which You inspired in St. Augustine, Your Bishop. Filled by this spirit, may we thirst after You as the true Source of wisdom.

Patron of Theologians

AUGUSTINE was born at Tagaste in North Africa in 354. His father was a pagan who wanted his son to be a man of learning, and cared little about his character. His mother was St. Monica, who urged her son to lead a good life. It was a common practice among Christians at that time to delay Baptism until later in life.

At sixteen, and still not baptized, Augustine fell into bad company. He read bad books. For thirteen years he led a very evil life.

Augustine often went to church to listen to St. Ambrose, the Archbishop of Milan, in Italy. But he was not converted. His mother, St. Monica, kept praying for her son.

One day while he was reading the letters of St. Paul, he made up his mind to become a Christian. His mother's prayers were answered. Augustine was baptized by St. Ambrose at the age of thirty-three. Later, Augustine became a priest and then a bishop. He preached and wrote many books during thirty-five years as bishop of Hippo in North Africa.

St. Augustine once wrote: "Our hearts were made for You, O Lord, and they are restless until they rest in You."

ROSE was born in Peru, South America. She was very obedient to her parents. She did all tasks with a happy smile. She always tried to do little things that were pleasing to others.

Rose was very pretty. Her mother wanted her to wear beautiful clothes. But Rose would say, "Mother, only beauty of the soul is worthwhile."

A rich young man wanted to marry Rose. He offered her a large home and many servants, but she refused. She wanted only to love and serve God.

When her parents had lost their money, Rose went out every day to work, and at night did sewing, to help her parents.

Rose visited the homes of the poor and brought them food. She offered all her sufferings and good works to God for sinners. Our Lord often appeared to her like a little child to tell her how pleased He was with her kind deeds.

Rose died in 1617 when she was only thirty-one years of age. She is the first saint of the Americas.

SAINT ROSE OF LIMA

August 23

O God, You filled St. Rose with love for You and enabled her to leave the world and be free for You through the austerity of penance. Through her intercession, help us to follow her footsteps on earth and enjoy the torrent of Your delights in heaven.

———

Patroness of South America

83

SAINT PIUS X

August 21

O God, to preserve the Catholic Faith and renew all things in Christ, You filled Pope St. Pius with heavenly wisdom and apostolic fortitude. Grant that we may follow his direction and example and be rewarded with eternal life with You.

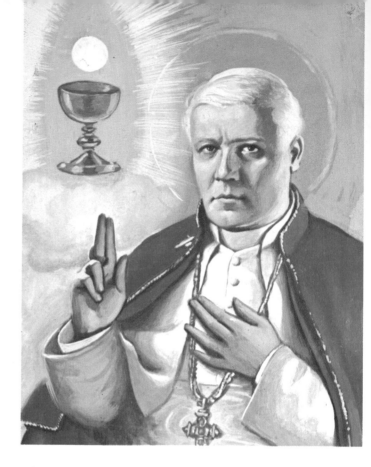

JOSEPH Sarto was the son of a poor village shoemaker and the oldest of eight children. Two priests of the parish helped him through school because he wanted to become a priest. He was very bright and a hard worker at the Padua seminary. After ordination he was made an assistant to the pastor in a small Italian town in the mountains. All the people loved him because he was kind. His soul was on fire with the love of God, especially when he preached about the Blessed Sacrament.

Later, when he became Bishop of Mantua, he said, "I shall spare myself neither care nor labor nor earnest prayers for the salvation of souls. My hope is in Christ."

Bishop Sarto was made a cardinal, and, when Pope Leo XIII died in 1903, he was elected Pope. His motto was: "To restore all things in Christ, so that Christ may be all in all." His teaching was: "Love God, and lead good Christian lives." He wanted this to come about through frequent Holy Communion. He died on August 20, 1914, with the words: "All things in Christ."

St. Pius X is called the Pope of the Blessed Sacrament.

PETER CLAVER was a Spanish Jesuit. He was sent to Cartagena in South America where he spent forty years in this great slave market of the West Indies, laboring for the salvation of African Negroes. He consecrated himself by vow to the salvation of those ignorant and miserable people, and he called himself "the slave of the slaves." He was their apostle, father, physician, and friend. When news arrived of a slave ship coming into port, Peter would go on board at once and bring comfort to his dear slaves. He fed and clothed them, and nursed them with the greatest tenderness in their ugly diseases. It is said that he baptized forty thousand Negro slaves before he went to his reward in 1654.

Peter would say, "We must speak to them (the Negroes) with our hands by giving, before we try to speak to them with our lips." He organized charitable societies among the Spanish people in Cartagena just as St. Vincent de Paul did in Paris.

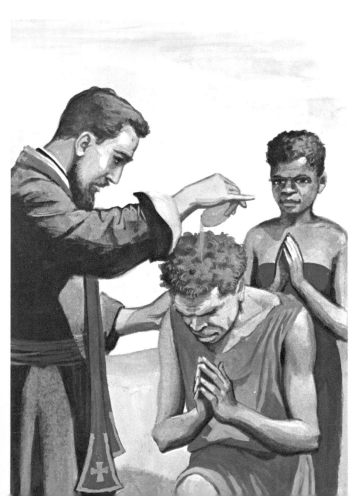

SAINT PETER CLAVER

September 9

O God, You conferred on St. Peter Claver a remarkable love and patience to help Your enslaved people and bring them to a knowledge of Your Name. Through his intercession, help us to seek equality for all races.

Patron of the
Negro Missions

SAINT MATTHEW THE EVANGELIST

September 21

O God, You chose St. Matthew the Publican to become an Apostle. By following his example and benefiting by his prayers, may we always follow and abide by Your will.

Patron of Bankers and Bookkeepers

MATTHEW, called Levi, was the son of Alphaeus. He lived at Capharnaum on Lake Genesareth.

The first Gospel was written by Matthew in which he speaks of his call to be an Apostle. Sitting at his desk one day, he saw Christ come to him. When the Lord said to him, "Follow Me," he at once left his work and followed the Master. The people were surprised to see a Roman tax collector become one of the special friends and disciples of the Master.

Matthew also tells us of the banquet he gave that Christ attended. It was a public farewell to his former friends. Many publicans and sinners came and sat down with Jesus and His disciples. Jesus said, "I have come not to call the just, but sinners."

Matthew wrote his Gospel to convince the Jews that the Messias had come in the Person of Jesus Christ. His symbol is a young man because he begins his Gospel with Christ's earthly ancestry and stresses His human and kingly character. He preached the Gospel among the Hebrews for fifteen years. He is also called the Apostle of Ethiopia. His shrine is at Salerno in Southern Italy.

BORN in France in 1607, Isaac Jogues had always wanted to become a missionary. He joined the Society of Jesus and was sent to New France, as Canada was then called. His joy was great as he stepped on shore in the New World. For years he had dreamed of leading the savage redskins to the feet of Christ.

Father Jogues and his companions suffered great hardships and were always in danger of death. Whenever anything went wrong among the Indians, the "Blackrobes" were blamed.

On an expedition to Quebec for supplies of medicine and food, Father Jogues and his companions were surrounded by a band of Iroquois, who were the most warlike of the Indian tribes. They were taken captive and were tortured without mercy for months.

When the French government tried to secure his freedom, Father Jogues wrote: "I prefer to remain as a captive unless it be the will of God that I escape." Later, he did escape and returned to France.

But Father Jogues again returned to the Indians. One evening he was seized in the wigwam of an Iroquois chief. His head was crushed with a tomahawk and he was scalped.

SAINT ISAAC JOGUES

October 19

O God, You consecrated the spread of the Faith in North America by the blood of St. Isaac Jogues and his companions who were preaching the Faith to the Indians. Through their intercession let more people everywhere respond to the Good News of salvation.

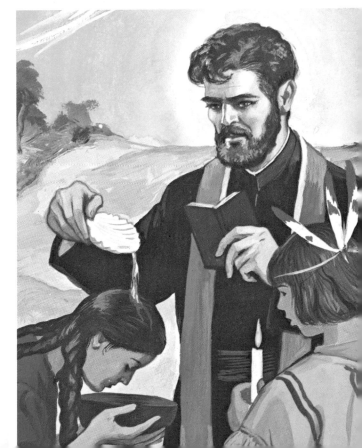

87

WHEN God created the angels, those beautiful spirits of light and love which surround His heavenly throne in great numbers, He gave them wonderful gifts of holiness, beauty and wisdom. God wanted to test them in their love for Him before they were to see Him face to face in the glory of heaven.

One of the greatest of the angels was Lucifer, whose name means "bearer of light." He was proud of his power and raised his battle cry of disobedience: "I will not serve God!"

But another great archangel set up his battle cry of love and obedience: *"Mi-cha-el—Who is like God?"* In a great battle the good angels cast the bad angels into hell. In reward for his love and obedience, God made Archangel Michael prince of all the heavenly armies.

From the beginning of time, St. Michael was the leader of God's chosen people. In the New Testament he is the guardian angel and the protector of the Catholic Church.

SAINT MICHAEL

September 29

O God, You arranged the services of angels and of men in a wonderful order. Mercifully grant that they who always stand before Your face ministering to You in heaven may also defend our life upon earth.

Patron of Policemen

SAINT JEROME

September 30

O God, You gave St. Jerome a great love for Holy Scripture. Let Your people feed more abundantly on Your word and find in it the source of life.

Patron of Librarians

JEROME, born in Dalmatia, was sent to school at Rome. He visited foreign cities, devoted himself to the sciences and oratory, and finally became a lawyer. For a time he lived a worldly life, but later he received baptism at Rome.

After traveling through the East and visiting many holy persons, he decided to live in the desert of Chalcis in Syria, where he spent four years in prayer, study and penance. He writes of himself: "My limbs were covered with sackcloth and my skin became dry. For fear of hell I retired here into the dwelling place of serpents and of wild animals." He once drew a thorn from a lion's paw; the animal in gratitude remained with him ever after.

Jerome became a priest at Antioch. He went to Palestine and joined a monastery at Bethlehem. He translated the Bible into Latin, which was to be his noblest work. For thirty years he wrote many learned works, especially about Holy Scripture, and preserved in Latin the writings of many learned men. When he died in the year 420, his body was buried at Bethlehem and later removed to Rome.

SAINT THERESE OF THE CHILD JESUS

October 1

O God our Father, You destined Your Kingdom for Your children who are humble. Help us to imitate the way of St. Theresa, so that, by her intercession, we may attain the eternal glory which You promised.

Patroness of Foreign Missions

WHEN Therese was eight years old she was cured because a statue of the Blessed Virgin smiled upon her.

When Therese was still very young she did kind little deeds for everyone. She prepared for her First Holy Communion by making many little sacrifices. She became a very special friend of Jesus. She once said, "From the age of three, I never refused our good God anything. I have never given Him anything but love."

Therese entered the Carmelite convent at the age of fifteen. She wanted to save souls, and to help priests save souls, by prayer, sacrifice, and suffering. Her "Little Way" means love and trust in God.

St. Therese is called the Little Flower of Jesus because she loved the Infant Jesus and, like a child, did little things to please God.

When she was dying, St. Therese pressed her crucifix to her heart and, looking up to heaven, she said, "I love Him! My God, I love You!" She was only twenty-four years old when she died in 1897.

SAINT FRANCIS OF ASSISI

October 4

O God, You enabled St. Francis to imitate Christ by his poverty and humility. Walking in St. Francis' footsteps, may we follow Your Son and be bound to You by a joyful love.

———

Patron of Catholic Action

AS a young man Francis liked to have a good time. His father was rich. But once, when he was sick, Francis heard our Lord calling him to leave the world and follow Him. Francis began to visit the hospitals and to serve the sick. He used to say, "When one serves the poor, he serves Christ Himself."

Francis put on the clothes of a poor shepherd and began to preach to the people about peace with God, peace with one's neighbor, and peace with one's self. He looked on all people and things as his brothers and sisters because they were all created by the same God.

Francis took twelve young men to Rome with him, and the Pope gave him permission to start a new religious order, the Franciscans. He also helped St. Clare to start the order known as the Poor Clares.

Francis had a vision in which he saw Jesus hanging on the Cross. The marks of the five wounds of Jesus were left in his hands, his side, and his feet, which remained with him all his life.

When Francis became very ill, he prayed, "O Lord, I thank You for the pains which I suffer." He died October 4, 1226.

SAINT BRIDGET

July 23

Lord God, You revealed heavenly secrets to St. Bridget as she meditated on the Passion of Your Son. Grant that we Your servants may attain the joyful contemplation of Your glory.

———

Patroness of Sweden

BRIDGET was born of a Swedish royal family in the year 1304. In obedience to her father, she was married to Prince Ulpho of Sweden, and became the mother of eight children, one of whom, Catherine, is honored as a saint.

In order to live an even holier life, she and her husband agreed to separate. He entered the Cistercian Order, and Bridget founded the Order of St. Savior, or the Brigittines, in Sweden. She later made a pilgrimage to Rome and Palestine because she had a great love for the Passion of Christ. She encouraged the nuns in her convent to practice the same devotion.

Bridget was patient in bearing the sufferings of her illness for the love of Jesus on the Cross. Her son and daughter, Catherine, were with her in her last moments. She died in Rome in the year 1373.

St. Bridget teaches us to love Jesus Crucified. Thinking of His Passion and death will help us to understand still better the love of God for us, and the evil of mortal sin.

SAINT EDWARD

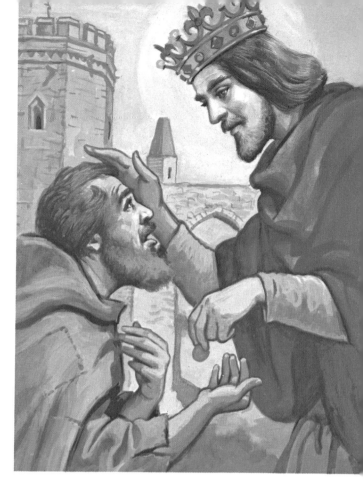

January 5

O God, You crowned St. Edward with the glory of eternity. May we venerate him on earth so that we may be able to reign with him in heaven.

EDWARD was raised to the throne of England at the age of forty years, twenty-seven of which he had passed in exile. Though he married to satisfy his people, he lived in continence with his wife, Edith.

One of the noblemen at his palace wrote: "Edward was a man by choice devoted to God, living the life of an angel in ruling his kingdom, and therefore was directed by God. He was so gentle that he would not say an unkind word even to the meanest person."

Edward was generous to the poor and strangers. He used to stand at his palace gate, speaking kindly to the poor beggars and lepers who crowded about him, many of whom he healed of their diseases. No matter how busy he was, he would be present at Mass daily. The holy king had a great devotion to building and enriching churches. Westminster Abbey was his last work. He died on January 5, 1065. In 1611 he was canonized, and two years later his incorrupt body was taken to a shrine of the Abbey by St. Thomas Becket.

SAINT TERESA OF AVILA

October 15

O God, You raised up St. Teresa by Your Spirit so that she could manifest to the Church the way to perfection. Nourish us with the food of her heavenly teaching, and fire us with a desire for holiness. ___

Patroness against
Headaches

TERESA was the daughter of noble parents in Spain. When she was only seven years of age she and her little brother liked to read stories from the lives of the saints. One of their favorite games was playing "hermit" in their father's garden.

When Teresa was still quite young, she became crippled by disease and was unable to walk. She prayed to St. Joseph, who cured her.

Teresa lost her mother when she was twelve. She begged the Mother of God to be her mother. Five years after her mother's death she joined the Carmelite Order. She built many new convents.

By a life of constant prayer, Teresa brought many souls to Jesus. Her many writings show her great love of God.

Teresa wrote these beautiful words: "Let nothing trouble you, let nothing make you afraid. All things pass away. God never changes. Patience obtains everything. God alone is enough."

On October 4, 1582, Jesus appeared to Teresa with many saints. She begged Him to take her to Himself. After her prayer, her soul was taken to heaven.

GERARD was born in Muro, Italy, on April 23, 1726. His father, a tailor, died when the boy was twelve, leaving the family in poverty.

Gerard could not join the Capuchins because of ill health, but he was accepted by the Redemptorists as a lay brother. He served as sacristan, gardener, porter, infirmarian and tailor.

Even during his life Gerard was called "the wonder-worker" because so many miraculous things happened through his intercession. He was given extraordinary knowledge. He had a heroic spirit of penance which caused him to suffer in silence when falsely accused of immoral conduct by an evil woman who later confessed her lie. Because of this or because he helped a woman on the verge of childbirth, he is invoked as a patron of expectant mothers.

Gerard died of tuberculosis in 1755 at the age of twenty-nine. His last request was that this small note be tacked to his door: "Here the will of God is done, as God wills, and as long as God wills." Brother Gerard was canonized by Pope St. Pius X, December 11, 1904.

SAINT GERARD MAJELLA

October 16

O God, by Your grace, St. Gerard persevered in imitating Christ in His poverty and humility. Through his intercession, grant that we may faithfully follow our vocation and reach that perfection which You held out to us in Your Son. ___

Patron of Expectant Mothers

ST. Margaret Mary was born in 1647 in France. She was a cripple, but the Blessed Virgin cured her. In thanksgiving she promised to give her life to God. When she was seventeen, Jesus appeared to her, just as He was after He was scourged. She decided at once to enter the Order of the Visitation.

Sister Margaret Mary loved our Lord in the Blessed Sacrament very much. He showed her His Sacred Heart in four visions. The flames that come forth from His Heart symbolize His burning love for us and His desire that we love Him in return. The crown of thorns around His Heart symbolizes sacrifice to make up for sin.

Jesus made at least twelve promises to her. Some of those promises are: that He would bless those who honor His Sacred Heart, that He would give them all the graces they need, that He would give them the favor of dying in the state of grace if they received Communion on nine First Fridays.

Jesus said to her: "Look at this Heart which has loved men so much, and yet men do not want to love Me in return. Through you My divine Heart wishes to spread its love everywhere on earth."

SAINT MARGARET MARY ALACOQUE

October 16

O Lord, pour out upon us the spirit with which You enriched St. Margaret Mary. Help us to know the love of Christ which is too great for human knowledge and to be filled with the fullness of God.

SAINT LUKE THE EVANGELIST

October 18

O God, You chose St. Luke to reveal in preaching and writing Your love for the poor. Grant that those who already glory in Your Name may persevere in one heart and one mind, and that all people may hear Your Good News of salvation. ___

Patron of Painters and Physicians

LUKE was born at Antioch, Syria. He was a Greek by birth and a physician by profession. He was skillful in painting, for some Greeks speak of his leaving many pictures of Jesus and Mary.

Luke was one of the earliest converts to the Faith. Later he became the missionary companion of St. Paul on part of his second and third missionary journeys. He attended Paul during his imprisonment in Caesarea and Rome. Paul refers to him as "the most dear physician" and "a fellow-laborer." He sailed with Paul and Silas from Troas to Macedonia, stayed behind for seven years at Philippi, and shared the shipwreck and perils of the voyage to Rome. From Paul's Epistles we learn that Luke was his faithful companion to the end.

Luke is the author of the third Gospel, written before the year 63. He also wrote the *Acts of the Apostles*. His symbol is the ox, the animal of sacrifice, because he begins his Gospel with the history of Zachary the priest, offering sacrifice to God. He speaks of the priesthood of Christ. He also speaks about the wonderful works of God in beginning His Church, and about St. Paul's actions and miracles which he himself witnessed.

97

SAINT ANTHONY MARY CLARET

October 24

O God, You strengthened St. Anthony Mary with wondrous love and patience in evangelizing the people. Through his intercession, enable us to seek those things which are Yours, and to labor in Christ for the good of our fellow men.

ANTHONY was born at Sallent, Spain, in 1807. He labored as a missionary in Catalonia and the Canary Islands for ten years, giving missions and retreats. His zeal inspired other priests to join in the same work, and in 1849 he founded the Congregation of Missionary Sons of the Immaculate Heart of Mary. The institute is known by his name as "the Claretians."

Father Claret was appointed Archbishop of Santiago in Cuba. His work for the church was harmed by men who tried to take his life. Here he founded the Teaching Sisters of Mary Immaculate.

At the request of Pope Pius IX, he returned to Spain and devoted himself to missionary work and the spreading of good literature. In the course of his life he is said to have preached ten thousand sermons and to have published two hundred books or pamphlets for both priests and people. He spread devotion to the Blessed Sacrament and the Immaculate Heart of Mary by his preaching and writings. His union with God was rewarded by many favors and cures.

St. Anthony died in a Cistercian monastery in France on October 24, 1870. He was canonized by Pope Pius XII.

RAPHAEL first appeared in Holy Scripture in the Book of Tobit. He called himself "Azariah" when, in human form, he became the traveling companion of the young Tobiah on his journey to Rages. Tobiah was going to this city in the country of the Medes to collect a debt owed to his father. Raphael kept Tobiah from all danger and brought him back safely to his father's house. He also found a very good wife for the young man, and cured his father's blindness with the gall taken from the fish Tobiah had killed. The angel then made himself known in these words: "I am the Archangel Raphael, one of the seven spirits who stand before the throne of God."

They all wondered why God sent them an angel. Raphael replied, "Because you have always worshiped God, buried the dead, were kind to the poor, bore your troubles bravely, God sent me to you. Praise the Lord of heaven who has shown you His mercy!"

The name Raphael means "God has healed." St. Raphael is the patron of travelers, physicians, and young people, especially to help them in their vocation. He is called the angel of love and joy.

SAINT RAPHAEL THE ARCHANGEL

September 29

O God, You gave St. Raphael, the Archangel, to Your servant Tobiah as a companion on his journey. Grant that we may always be protected by his care and strengthened by his help.

———

Patron of Travelers

SAINT JUDE THADDEUS

October 28

O God, You made Your Name known to us through the Apostles. By the intercession of St. Jude, let Your Church continue to grow with an increased number of believers.

———

Patron of Desperate Cases

JUDE Thaddeus was a nephew of Mary and Joseph, and a cousin of our Lord. He was a brother of the Apostle James the Less. His father was Cleophas, who died a martyr, and his mother's name was Mary. She stood beneath the Cross when Jesus died, and later came to anoint the body of Jesus.

In his boyhood and youth Jude must have known Jesus well. He left all to follow the Master.

Jude is sometimes pictured with an image of our Lord because he cured the King of Edessa from leprosy in the name of Jesus.

God gave Jude a special power. When he ordered the devils in pagan idols to leave, the images fell to the ground, broken into pieces.

Jude and Simon suffered martyrdom in Persia, where they labored as missionaries. Jude was beaten to death with a club. His head was then cut from his body with an ax. His relics are now honored in St. Peter's Basilica in Rome. St. Jude is very popular as the patron of impossible cases.

SAINT CHARLES BORROMEO

November 4

O God, maintain in Your people that spirit with which You inspired Your Bishop, St. Charles, so that Your Church may be constantly renewed, conforming itself to Christ and manifesting Christ to the world.

Patron of Seminarians and Catechists

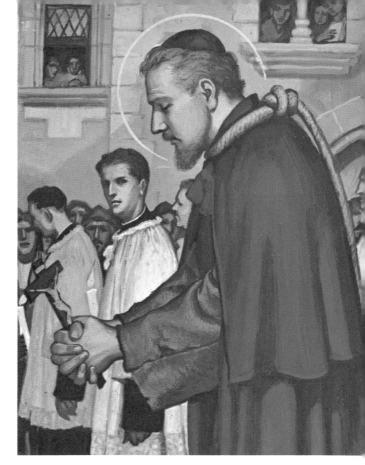

CHARLES, of the noble family of Borromeo, was born on October 2, 1538, in a castle of Aron, in Italy. He received a doctor's degree in law at twenty-one. Pius IV created him cardinal and nominated him archbishop of Milan, though he was only twenty-two.

Charles became a great reformer and, more than anyone else, helped the Church during the storm caused by Martin Luther during the Reformation. His great work was the direction of the Council of Trent, and the carrying out of its decrees. He founded schools for the poor, seminaries for clerics, and through his community of Oblates trained his priests to holiness of life. He instructed St. Aloysius Gonzaga, heard his confession, and gave him his first Holy Communion.

Charles founded hospitals where he himself served the sick. He slept on straw or boards and lived on black bread, chestnuts and dried figs. He was often seen taking part in public processions with a rope around his neck as a sign of penance. He gave away all his belongings and wore an old patched cloak. During the great plague, he was ever with the sick and dying. He died in 1584.

St. Charles is the patron saint of seminarians and catechists.

SAINT MARTIN DE PORRES

November 3

O God, You led St. Martin by the way of humility to heavenly glory. Help us to follow the example of his holiness and so become worthy to be exalted with him in heaven.

MARTIN was born in Lima, Peru, in 1579, of a Spanish father and a Negro, or Indian, mother. He grew up in poverty and had a deep understanding and love for the poor.

When quite young, he went to work for a surgeon-barber where he learned about medicine and how to care for the sick and the wounded.

At the age of fifteen, Martin entered the Dominican convent in Lima as a helper. Later he became a lay brother. With joy and generosity he performed lowly tasks in the kitchen, laundry, wardrobe room, and infirmary. His charity knew no bounds as he helped those in need of food or a word of encouragement. He loved all God's creatures, even the lowly mice which did so much damage to the convent linens!

Blessed with the gift of healing, Martin once cured the ailing Archbishop of Mexico with a touch of the hand.

Martin died of a fever in 1639, and was beatified in 1873. On May 6, 1962 he was canonized by Pope John XXIII.

SAINT STANISLAUS KOSTKA

August 15

Lord God, You alone are holy and no one is good without You. Thrugh the intercession of St. Stanislaus Kostka help us to live in such a way that we may not be deprived of a share in Your glory.

S TANISLAUS was born in 1550 of a noble Polish family. At fourteen he attended the college of the Jesuits at Vienna with his elder brother Paul. Though Stanislaus was always bright and kind, he was mistreated for two years by his brother. Stanislaus became very ill but, being in the house of a Lutheran, he could not call for a priest. He appealed to his patroness, St. Barbara. She appeared to him with two angels, who gave him the Sacred Host. He was cured by Our Lady herself, who asked him to enter the Society of Jesus. Stanislaus had to flee from Vienna because his father opposed his plans.

At Rome, Stanislaus did humble tasks cheerfully at the Jesuit College where he met St. Peter Canisius. He lived for ten months as a saintly novice. The Rule of his Order was so sacred to him that he carried a copy of it, written in his own hand, over his heart.

A priest said to him, "Stanislaus, you seem to love Our Lady very much." "Yes," he replied, "She is my Mother!" And then he added, "The Mother of God is *my* Mother."

Stanislaus died, as he had prayed to die, on the feast of the Assumption, 1568, at the age of seventeen.

SAINT ELIZABETH

November 17

O God, You taught St. Elizabeth to recognize and serve Christ in the poor. Grant, through her intercession, that we may always loving-ly serve the needy and the oppressed.

Patroness of Hospitals

ELIZABETH was a princess of Hungary. At the age of thirteen she married Prince Louis. As her castle stood on a steep rock, she built a hospital at the foot of the mountain. There she fed the poor and the sick daily and attended to their needs with her own hands. They loved her and called her "Dear St. Elizabeth."

When the ladies of the castle tried to keep her from going to help the poor, she said, "I am preparing for my judgment. I want to be able to say to Jesus: Jesus, when You were hungry, I gave You to eat; when You had nothing to put on, I clothed You; when You were sick, I visited You, because You said that in doing these things for the poor, I did them for You. I beg you to be kind to me."

One day Elizabeth was carrying bread for the poor. Her husband met her, and looking under the mantle saw only roses.

After her husband's death Elizabeth was left with four children. Giving her money to the poor, she worked to support her family.

Elizabeth died in 1302 at the age of twenty-four. Her last words were: "O Mary, come to help me." She is the patron of hospitals.

CECILIA was a member of a noble family of Rome and a follower of Christ. Her parents forced her to marry a nobleman named Valerian. In the evening of her wedding day, with the music of the marriage feast ringing in her ears, Cecilia renewed the vow by which she had consecrated her virginity to God. "Pure be my heart and undefiled my body; for I have a spouse you do not know, an angel of my Lord." This is why she is honored as a patron of music.

Cecilia converted her husband to the Faith of Christ. Because he helped Cecilia in her charity toward the poor, he was put to death. Cecilia refused to sacrifice to the gods. The judge condemned her to be smothered by steam. But God protected Cecilia. Then the judge ordered a soldier to kill her with the sword. He struck her three times, but did not cut off her head. She fell down, badly wounded, and for three days she remained alive. She gave her property to the holy Bishop Urban for the use of the Church, and received the sacrament of Holy Communion before she died. This happened in 117.

Cecilia was buried in the catacombs. Her grave was discovered in 817, and her body was placed in the church of St. Cecilia in Rome. In 1599, when her tomb was opened her body was incorrupt.

SAINT
CECILIA

November 22

O Lord, hear our requests. Through the intercession of Cecilia, please grant what we ask.

Patroness of Musicians

SAINT JOHN OF THE CROSS

December 14

O God, Your Priest St. John became a model of perfect self-denial and showed us how to love the Cross. May we always imitate him and be rewarded with the eternal contemplation of Your glory.

JOHN was born in Spain in 1542. His parents were very poor. He became the servant of the poor in the hospital of Medina. At twenty-one he became a lay brother at a Carmelite monastery where he practiced severe penance. His superiors, knowing his talents, sent him to Salamanca for higher studies, and he was ordained priest.

He met St. Teresa of Avila, who interested him in the work of reforming his own Order. Thus he became the first prior of the Discalced or barefoot Carmelites, and took the name of John of the Cross. Some of the friars rejected the reform and cast him into prison. After nine months of suffering, he escaped. On two other occasions he was publicly disgraced.

John wrote, "Live in the world as if only God and your soul were in it; then your heart will never be made captive by any earthly thing." Since he was always united to God in sincerest love, he bore his sufferings patiently. He died in 1591.

St. John was one of the great contemplatives. He was declared a Doctor of the Church.

SAINT CATHERINE LABOURE

November 25

Lord Jesus Christ, You were pleased to gladden the holy Virgin Catherine by the wonderful apparition of Your Immaculate Mother. Grant that by following the example of this saint we may obtain the joy of eternal life.

CATHERINE was born in 1806 in Burgundy, France. She was the ninth of eleven children. She refused many offers of marriage, and said, "I found my Bridegroom on the day of my First Communion. To Him alone have I given myself."

Catherine once paid a visit to a hospital which was in the care of the Sisters of Charity. In the parlor she saw a picture of St. Vincent de Paul and she heard the words, "My child, it is a very beautiful thing to take care of the sick. God is asking something from you." She later became a "Daughter of St. Vincent de Paul."

On the 18th of July, 1830, Catherine had a vision of Our Lady in which she described the miraculous medal, which has the image of Our Lady on one side with the words: "O Mary, conceived without sin, pray for us who have recourse to thee," and on the other side the Hearts of Jesus and Mary. Our Lady said, "Have a medal struck according to this model. Those who wear it will receive great graces." Three times the Virgin Mary appeared to Catherine, who was then a a twenty-four-year-old novice. Devotion to the miraculous medal spread rapidly throughout the world. Catherine died in 1876.

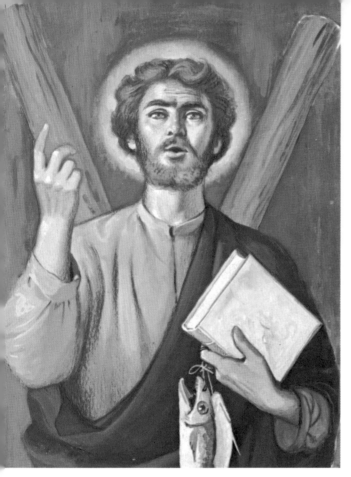

SAINT ANDREW

November 30

O Lord, You raised up St. Andrew, Your Apostle to preach and rule in Your Church. Grant that we may always experience the benefit of his intercession with You.

———

Patron of Fishermen

ONE day John the Baptist and two of his disciples, one of them being Andrew, saw Jesus walk by. John said, "Behold the Lamb of God!" And the two disciples followed Jesus.

They asked, "Where do You live, Master?" and Jesus said, "Come and see."

They stayed with Jesus that day. Later Andrew told his brother Peter, "We have found the Messias." And he led him to Jesus.

One day Jesus said to Peter and Andrew, "Go to the deep water and let down your nets."

"Master," said Peter, "we have been fishing all night, but have caught nothing."

But they let down their net. The net caught so many fishes that Peter and Andrew could not pull it up. They had to call for help.

Jesus said, "Follow Me, and I will make you fishers of men." And at once they gave up their work and followed Jesus.

Andrew preached the Gospel in Greece, and even in Russia and Poland. He was put to death on a cross, made in the form of an X.

SAINT FRANCIS XAVIER

December 3

O Lord, You won many peoples for Your Church through the preaching of St. Francis. Inspire the faithful today with the same zeal for spreading the Faith, so that everywhere the Church might rejoice in her many children.

Patron of Foreign Missions

FRANCIS was born in 1506 in Spain of noble parents. He was sent to the College of St. Barbara in Paris and became a teacher. He joined St. Ignatius Loyola and four other young men who vowed to work for the conversion of souls. They formed the Society of Jesus.

Before his ordination to the priesthood in Venice, he cared for the sick in a hospital. The King of Portugal wanted six missionaries to preach the Faith in India. One of these was Francis. He journeyed to Goa. There he comforted the sick and walked through the streets ringing a bell, asking the children to come to catechism in the church. Later he preached in public, and soon the whole city was converted. In the south of India he converted thousands of pagans. The burning flame coming forth from his heart is a sign of his burning love for souls. The globe reminds us that he traveled great distances to save them. He is the patron of the foreign missions.

Francis sailed for Japan in 1549. Other missionaries joined him there. He converted many thousands of people. While on a ship going to China, he became very ill of a high fever. The ship stopped at an island, off the coast. He died in an old cabin on December 2, 1552.

BARBARA was brought up a heathen. She was a very beautiful young woman, and many princes came to ask her father for her hand in marriage. But she refused to marry. Her father built a tower in which he jealously guarded his daughter. She gave herself to prayer and study, and managed to receive instruction and Baptism secretly.

When her father discovered her conversion, he was so angry that he drew his sword to kill her, but God delivered her. Later, her father brought her before a civil judge. The judge said to her, "Choose either to offer to the gods or be put to death by cruel torments." Barbara answered, "I offer myself to my God, Jesus Christ, who created Heaven and earth and all things."

After Barbara was beaten, our Lord came to comfort her in a vision. The judges ordered her to be slain with the sword. But her father came for her and took her to a mountain, where he himself beheaded her while she was praying to God to have mercy on his soul. Suddenly, fire came from heaven and consumed her father.

Barbara was martyred in the year 235. She is invoked against lightning and fire.

SAINT BARBARA

December 4

O God, You give us joy each year when we celebrate the feast of St. Barbara. May she inspire us by her example of courage and chastity and help us by her prayers.

———

Patroness of Prisoners

SAINT NICHOLAS

December 6

We call upon Your mercy, O Lord. Through the intercession of St. Nicholas, keep us safe amid all dangers so that we may go forward without hindrance on the road of salvation.

———

Patron of Bakers

NICHOLAS was born toward the end of the third century. He was ordained a priest, and appointed abbot of a monastery.

Nicholas was very generous to the poor. He showed himself the special protector of the innocent and the wronged. Once he heard that a man who had become very poor intended to abandon his three daughters to a life of sin. He went out by night, flung a bag of gold into the window of the sleeping father, and hurried away. Later the father fell at his feet and said, "Nicholas, you are my helper. You have delivered my soul and my daughters' from hell."

St. Nicholas is regarded as the special patron of children; the word Santa Claus comes from his name. He died at Myra in the year 342.

The Emperor Justinian built a church in his honor at Constantinople about the year 540. In 1807 his relics were brought to Bari, Italy. He has always been venerated in the Latin and Greek Churches. But the Russian Church seems to honor him more than any other saint. He is the patron saint of Russia.

SAINT AMBROSE

December 7

O God, by your grace St. Ambrose, Your Bishop, became a great teacher of the Catholic Faith and an example of apostolic fortitude. Raise up Bishops in Your Church today who will give strong and wise leadership.

Patron of Candle-Makers

AMBROSE was born in Gaul about the year 340. He was of a noble family. He received a good education in Rome and became a poet and a famous speaker. When he moved to Milan he was appointed Governor. The voice of a child marked him out to the people of Milan as their Bishop, at the age of thirty-four.

Ambrose gave his riches to the Church and to the poor. He was an eager student of the Holy Scriptures and the writers of the Church. He defended the Church against the Arian heretics of his time, and led the Emperor Theodosius and his queen to penance.

As a young man, St. Augustine heard him speak and was converted by his sermons. He admitted Augustine to the Church. Ambrose was an example of a zealous shepherd of souls. His heart was filled with a gentle love for the poor.

Ambrose died in the year 397. He left us many important writings on the doctrines of our Holy Faith. The Church honors him as one of her greatest Doctors and defenders. This is the reason why he is pictured holding a church in his hand. The beehive means wisdom.

SAINT LUCY

December 13

O Lord, may the intercession of Your Virgin and Martyr St. Lucy help us so that, as we celebrate her heavenly birthday on earth, we may contemplate her triumph in heaven.

Patron of Eye Patients

AT an early age Lucy offered herself to God. The rich young man who wanted to marry her was so angry at her refusal that he accused her of being a Christian .

About the year 304, Lucy was led to the governor of her city for trial. Unable to make her give up her Faith, he asked, "Is this Holy Spirit in you?" Lucy answered, "They whose hearts are pure are the temples of the Holy Spirit."

The governor spoke angrily, "But I will make you fall into sin, and the Holy Spirit will leave you." She replied, "I will never sin, so that the Holy Spirit will give me a greater reward."

Nothing could make her commit sin. She said, "You see now that I am the temple of the Holy Spirit, and that He protects me."

The governor ordered a fire to be lighted around her, but Lucy was not harmed. At last, a sword was buried in her heart. She did not die until a priest came to her with Holy Communion.

St. Lucy is invoked by people who have trouble with their eyes.

113

SAINT THOMAS THE APOSTLE

July 3

Almighty God, let us proudly rejoice as we celebrate the feast of St. Thomas the Apostle. May we be helped by his patronage and, believing, have life in the Name of Jesus Christ Your Son Whom he confessed to be the Lord. ___

Patron of Architects

THOMAS was called Didymus, which means the twin. He was a man of great courage and self-sacrifice. When Jesus told His disciples that He would return to Judea to visit His friend Lazarus, the Apostles knew that people would try to stone Him. But Thomas said to his companions, "Let us also go, that we may die with Him."

After the Resurrection, the Apostles said to Thomas, "We have seen the Lord." But he said, "Unless I see in His hands the print of the nails, and put my finger into the place of the nails, and put my hand into His side, I will not believe."

After eight days, Thomas was with the Apostles. Jesus came, the door being closed, and stood before Thomas and said, "Bring here your finger, and see My hands; and bring here your hand, and put it into My side; and be not unbelieving, but believing."

Thomas answered, "My Lord, and my God!" And Jesus said to him, "Because you have seen Me, Thomas, you have believed. Blessed are they who have not seen, and yet have believed."

After the Ascension, Thomas preached the Gospel in Parthia. He is also called the Apostle of the Indies, where he was martyred!

SAINT STEPHEN

December 26

O God, grant that we may imitate the saint we honor and learn to love our enemies. For today we celebrate the feast of St. Stephen who knew how to pray even for his persecutors.

Patron of Stonemasons

THE Apostles told the disciples to choose seven men who lived a holy life to help in the care of the poor. These men were called deacons, and Stephen was named first of the deacons. The Apostles ordained them deacons by praying and placing their hands upon them.

Stephen was full of grace and courage, and worked great wonders among the people. But some of the Jews accused him of talking against God and against Moses. He was brought before the court of the Jews. Stephen talked with great wisdom. People said there was a halo around his head and his face looked like that of an angel as he spoke bravely of Jesus Christ.

The Jews became very angry. But Stephen being full of the Holy Spirit, looking up to heaven, said, "I see the heavens opened and the Son of Man standing on the right hand of God."

The angry people dragged the holy deacon outside of the city and stoned him to death. But Stephen forgave his murderers. Falling upon his knees, he cried with a loud voice, "Lord, lay not this sin against them." When he said "Lord Jesus receive my spirit," he died. He was the first martyr.

SAINT JOHN, THE EVANGELIST

December 27

O God, through St. John the Apostle You willed to unlock to us the secrets of Your Word. Grant that what he has so excellently poured into our ears, we may properly understand.

———

Patron of Asia Minor

OUT of the twelve Apostles, Jesus chose three—Peter, James, and John—to be His most faithful companions.

John was the youngest of the twelve. He and his brother James had been followers of John the Baptist. But Jesus saw them one day helping their father mend fish nets. He called to them, "Come, follow Me!" And from that time on they stayed close to Him.

Jesus called them "sons of thunder" because they wished to call down fire on the town which would not receive their Master. Jesus was pleased to see them so zealous for His honor.

At the Last Supper, John rested his head on the shoulder of Jesus. He stayed with Jesus during His Passion and death, especially to console Mary. Jesus intrusted His own Mother to his care.

John preached in Palestine for many years. Later he was taken as a prisoner to Rome. He was thrown into a pot of boiling oil, but God kept him from harm. When he was ninety years old, he wrote his Gospel to prove that Jesus was God as well as man. His symbol is the eagle because he soars above the things of the earth and speaks of the divine nature of Christ.

116

SAINT ELIZABETH ANN SETON

January 4

O God, You raised up St. Elizabeth in Your Church so that she might instruct others in the way of salvation. Grant us so to follow Christ after her example that we may reach You in the company of our brothers.

BORN in New York City, August 28, 1774, Elizabeth lost her mother early, and her education became the concern of her father, Dr. Richard Bayley. She was very devout, fond of reading the Scriptures, and had a deep trust in Divine Providence.

At nineteen, Elizabeth married William Magee Seton of New York. Five children were born of their happy union. After her husband's death, the Felicchi—life-long friends—welcomed the grieving widow to their home in Italy, where Elizabeth found true Catholic life.

Elizabeth returned to New York in 1804 and entered the Catholic Church on March 14, 1805. She accepted an invitation from Archbishop Carroll to establish a girl's school in Baltimore. Several women joined her in the religious life, and she became known as "Mother Seton." They were known as Sisters of Charity and lived in Emmitsburg. This was the origin of six American communities of Sisters.

A school opened for the children of the parish was the first parochial school in the United States. Elizabeth died on January 4, 1821. In 1963 she became the first American-born citizen to be beatified and on September 14, 1975 she was canonized by Paul VI.

SAINT PIUS V

April 30

O God, You providently raised up St. Pius in Your Church for the defense of the Faith and for more suitable Divine worship. Through his intercession, help us to participate in Your mysteries with a livelier Faith and a more fruitful love.

DURING his papacy (1566-1572), Pius V was faced with the great responsibility of getting a scattered Church back on its feet. The family of God had been shaken by corruption, by the Reformation, by the constant threat of Turkish invasion, and by dissension.

Pius V was charged with the task of carrying out the sweeping reforms called for by the Council of Trent, which lasted 18 years. He ordered the founding of seminaries for the proper training of priests, published a new Missal, Breviary, and Catechism, and established the Confraternity of Christian Doctrine (CCD) classes for the young.

This saintly Pontiff also served the sick and the poor by building hospitals and providing food for the hungry. He spent long hours with his God in prayer, fasted, and deprived himself of many papal luxuries —all patterned after his previous life as a Dominican.

Only at the last minute was Pius able to organize a fleet which won a decisive victory against the Turks in the Gulf of Lepanto, off Greece on October 7, 1571. His pontificate was one of great renewal in the Church. He died in 1572.

SAINT JOHN NEPOMUCENE NEUMANN

January 5

O God, Light and Shepherd of souls, You established St. John as Bishop in Your Church to feed Your flock by his word and form it by his example. Help us through his intercession to keep the Faith he taught by his word and follow the way he showed us by his example.

JOHN Neumann was born in what is now Czechoslovakia. After studying in Prague, he came to New York at 25 and was ordained a priest. He did missionary work in New York State until he was 29, when he joined the Redemptorists and became the first in this Order to profess vows in the United States.

He continued to do missionary work in Maryland, Virginia, and Ohio, where he became popular with the Germans. He served in parishes in New York, Baltimore, and Pittsburgh and later became vice provincial of the American Redemptorists.

He became Bishop of Philadelphia in 1852 at 41. Gifted with outstanding organizing ability, he drew into the city many teaching Orders of Sisters and the Christian Brothers. While he was Bishop more than 80 churches were built.

John knew eight Slavic dialects and modern languages, and he traveled through his vast diocese by canal boat, stagecoach, railway, and on foot in his quest for souls. He was a pioneer in organizing the parochial school system and wrote a catechism. He died in 1860 performing his duties, and was canonized on July 19, 1977.

BARNABAS, a Jew of Cyprus, was closely associated with St. Paul. He introduced Paul to Peter and the other Apostles.

When a Christian community began at Antioch, Barnabas was sent as the official representative of the mother church of Jerusalem to unite its members in the fold of Christ. He and Paul gave instructions in Antioch for a year.

Later, Paul and Barnabas were sent by Antioch officials to preach to the Gentiles. Great success crowned their efforts. But all was not peaceful. They were expelled from some towns. Later Barnabas took Mark to Cyprus, and Paul took Silas to Syria.

Barnabas is spoken of simply as one who dedicated his life to the Lord. He was a man filled with the Holy Spirit and faith, through whom large numbers were added to the Lord's followers. Barnabas died a martyr at Cyprus during Nero's reign with the Gospel of St. Matthew, written by his own hand, on his chest.

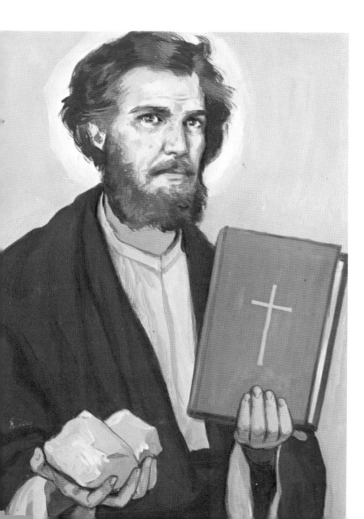

SAINT BARNABAS

June 11

O God, You commanded that St. Barnabas, who was full of Faith and the Holy Spirit, should be set apart to labor for the conversion of the Gentiles. May Christ's Gospel which he preached with great ardor continue to be preached faithfully by word and deed.

SAINT MARTIN OF TOURS

November 11

O God, Your Bishop St. Martin glorified You by both his life and his death. Renew in us Your grace, so that neither death nor life can separate us from Your love.

Patron of Soldiers

MARTIN was born of pagan parents in what is now Hungary around the year 316 and was raised in Italy. The son of a Roman officer, he was forced to serve in the army at the age of 15. He became a Christian catechumen, and was baptized at 18.

On a cold day, the legend goes, Martin met a poor man, almost naked, trembling, and begging from passersby. Martin had nothing but weapons and clothes. He drew his sword, cut his cloak into two pieces, and gave one to the beggar. That night in his sleep Martin saw Christ dressed in the half of the garment he had given away, and heard Him say: "Martin, still a catechumen, has covered Me with his garment."

At 23, Martin was discharged and went to be a disciple of St. Hilary of Poitiers, France. He was ordained a priest and after a brief exile, returned to France where he lived for 10 years, forming his disciples and preaching throughout the countryside.

The people of Tours demanded that he become their Bishop. He was the ideal good pastor, founding other monasteries, educating the clergy, and preaching the Gospel. He died in 397.

SAINT MAXIMILIAN KOLBE

August 14

Heavenly Father, You inflamed Blessed Maximilian the Priest with love for the Immaculate Virgin and filled him with zeal for souls and love for neighbor. Through his prayers grant us to work strenuously for Your glory in the service of others, and so be made conformable to Your Son until death.

BLESSED Maximilian Kolbe was born on January 7, 1894 in Poland and became a Franciscan. He contracted tuberculosis and, though he recovered, he remained frail all his life.

The year before his ordination as a priest, Father Kolbe founded the Immaculate Movement. After receiving a doctorate in theology, he spread the Movement through a magazine entitled "The Knight of the Immaculate" and helped form a community of 800 Franciscan men, the largest in the world.

He went to Japan where he built a comparable monastery and then on to India where he furthered the Movement. In 1936 he returned home because of unstable health. After the Nazi invasion in 1939, he was imprisoned and released for a time. But he was arrested again in 1941 and sent to the terrible concentration camp at Auschwitz.

On July 31, 1941, in reprisal for one prisoner's escape, ten men were chosen to die. One was a young husband and father. Father Kolbe offered himself in his place. He was the last to die, enduring two weeks of slow death through starvation, thirst, and neglect.

SAINT IGNATIUS OF ANTIOCH

October 17

Almighty and ever-living God, You adorn the body of Your holy Church with the witness of Your Martyrs. Grant that the sufferings of St. Ignatius on this day which brought unending glory to him may bring us perpetual protection.

BORN in Syria, Ignatius converted to Christianity and eventually became Bishop of Antioch. In the year 107 the Emperor Trajan visited Antioch and forced the Christians there to choose between death and apostasy. Ignatius would not deny Christ and thus was condemned to be put to death in Rome.

On the long journey to Rome, he wrote seven letters. Five of these letters are to Churches in Asia Minor and urge the Christians there to remain faithful to God and to obey their superiors.

The sixth letter was to Polycarp, Bishop of Smyrna, who was later martyred for the Faith. The final letter begs the Christians in Rome not to try to stop his martyrdom. "The only thing I ask of you is to allow me to offer the libation of my blood to God. I am the wheat of the Lord; may I be ground by the teeth of the beasts to become the pure bread of Christ. In the year 107 Ignatius bravely met the lions in the Coliseum.

Strengthened by the love of God, Ignatius showed great concern for the unity of the Church and steadfast fidelity to Christ.

SAINT MARIA SOLEDAD TORRES ACOSTA

October 11

God our Father, You called St. Maria Soledad to seek Your Kingdom in this world by striving to live in perfect charity. With her prayers to give us courage, help us to move forward with joyful hearts in the way of love.

SAINT Maria Soledad Torres Acosta, Foundress of the Congregation of Sisters Servants of Mary, Ministers of the Sick, was born in Madrid, Spain, on December 2, 1826. She met Father Miguel Martinez Sanz who wanted to found a Congregation of women devoted to Mary and dedicated to care for the sick, especially in their homes.

On August 15, 1851, Maria Soledad and six other young women began their religious life. Five years after the foundation of the Sisterhood, Maria Soledad was appointed superior and held the office with great efficiency. She gave proof of great charity, meekness, and humility, virtues which attract and win the sincere love and devotion of the Sisters and also of the people.

Always united to God, she did everything for His greater glory and relied entirely on His help. To be more like Christ, she had to suffer misunderstandings and persecutions in her life.

Maria Soledad died in Madrid, October 11, 1887, and was canonized by Paul VI on January 25, 1970. Today the number of her Religious is more than 2,500 spread throughout twenty countries of the world.